HARMONY HOMESTEAD

Harmony Homestead

Collective Strength, Shared Joy

MACK RAFEAL

Mohammed Altaf Hussain

Contents

Table of Content

Chapter 5: "Celebrations of Togetherness"
5.1 Showcase of joyous family celebrations.
5.2 Shared memories of special occasions.
5.3 Illustration of how collective joy is amplified during festivities.

Chapter 6: "Crisis and Compassion"
6.1 Examination of how the family handles crises.
6.2 Stories of support and compassion during tough times.
6.3 Lessons learned from facing adversity together.

Chapter 7: "Legacy of Love"
7.1 Reflection on the family's journey.
7.2 Consideration of the legacy passed down through generations.
7.3 Final thoughts on the enduring power of collective strength and shared joy.

Introduction

In the peaceful hug of Congruity Estate, the actual embodiment of familial solidarity tracks down its foundations. This story looks to uncover the significant embroidery that ties ages together, winding around a story of aggregate strength and shared happiness that reverberates inside the walls of this dwelling place. In following the starting points of solidarity, it becomes clear that the family's ancestry fills in as the foundation whereupon their amicable presence is fabricated.

Installed inside the chronicles of time are accounts of flexibility, love, and shared encounters that have shaped Concordance Estate into a safehaven of aggregate strength. Ages have strolled similar foyers, shared chuckling in similar spaces, and faced life's hardships as one strong unit. It is inside the structure of this common history that the family tracks down the solidarity to confront the difficulties of the present and the vulnerabilities representing things to come.

The actual space of Congruity Property isn't only a design; a living demonstration of the solidarity characterizes the family. The common spaces, from the core of the home to the calm corners where stories are murmured, become observers to the ordinary orchestra of harmony. It is in these spaces that the family produces bonds, tracking down comfort in the basic demonstration of conjunction.

However, the solidarity of Congruity Residence reaches out past the actual domain. The immaterial string of customs winds through the ages, restricting hearts in a common embroidery of values and ceremonies. The customs become a musical heartbeat, throbbing through the family's shared perspective and conferring a feeling of personality and having a place. It is through the recognition of these practices that the family finds the delight in shared minutes as well as the strength got from regarding the tradition of the past.

Inside the hug of this aggregate strength, Congruity Property turns into a sanctuary for flexibility. Life's difficulties are not met in confinement but rather looked as a unified front. Through the back and forth movement of wins and afflictions, the family stands together, drawing strength from the resolute help that every part gives. It is at these times of difficulty that the genuine proportion of their aggregate backbone is uncovered, a demonstration of the power that solidarity holds in exploring life's capricious territory.

As jobs and obligations are woven into the texture of day to day existence, the family finds the sensitive harmony among singularity and shared obligation. Every part contributes an exceptional string to the familial embroidery, making a mosaic of qualities that join consistently.

The interconnectedness of jobs cultivates a feeling of reliance, where the outcome of one turns into the victory of all. In this fragile dance of liabilities, the family tracks down productivity as well as the magnificence of shared dependence.

In the effortlessness of their common presence, the family finds a getting through strength that opposes the intricacies of the world. It is a strength conceived out of the straightforward excellence of harmony, where the significant lies in the effortlessness of shared minutes. Inside the walls of Concordance Estate, there is an acknowledgment that euphoria isn't restricted to terrific signals yet is tracked down in the quietude of shared spaces and the delicate rhythm of shared chuckling.

The festivals that intersperse the family's process become energetic markers of their solidarity. Whether in the blissful reverberations of merriments or the common seriousness of ceremonies, the family tracks down delight in the demonstration of festivity itself. These minutes become the parts of an aggregate story, written in the language of shared encounters and scratched into the memory of Concordance Property. In the festival of solidarity, the family finds the enhancement of satisfaction, where shared joy turns into a permanent piece of their common story.

In the midst of the festivals, notwithstanding, lie the snapshots of emergency that test the obligations of the family. It is in these pots of misfortune that the genuine person of Concordance Property sparkles. The aggregate empathy and support that arise during seasons of difficulty become the paste that ties the family much more tight. The comprehension that they are in good company to confront difficulties develops a flexibility that rises above individual strength, drawing from the well of aggregate guts.

As the family explores the progression of time, the tradition of adoration and solidarity turns into a directing light. The reverberations of shared chuckling, the reverberation of shared stories, and the persevering through string of aggregate strength weave a story that reaches out past the present. The tradition of Concordance Estate isn't restricted to the walls of the actual construction; it lives on in the hearts of every age, passed down like a loved treasure.

1. **Introduction to the family's history and values.**
   Settled inside the pages of time, the historical backdrop of a family unfurls — a story woven with strings of adoration, versatility, and shared values. In this investigation, we dig into the foundations of a familial heritage that stretches across ages, making an embroidery of aggregate strength and shared euphoria. The excursion starts with a comprehension of the family's ancestry, a rich embroidery that shapes the actual pith of their personality.
   Ages have traveled every which way, making behind a permanent imprint on the genealogical record. The hereditary roots run profound, establishing the present in a continuum of encounters, customs, and stories.
   Every individual from the family is a living part in this continuous adventure, adding to the story that is molded by the decisions, battles, and wins of the people who preceded.
   The family's qualities act as the compass directing them through the flows of time. These qualities are not simple unique standards; they are lived, inhaled, and passed down starting with one age then onto the next. They structure the bedrock whereupon the family stands, giving a moral and moral system that rises above individual inclinations and sentiments. It is inside the cauldron of shared values that the family finds an aggregate personality — an ethical compass that steers them through life's heap difficulties.
   As we follow the family's ancestry, we experience accounts of strength that reverberation through the passages of time. The hardships looked by precursors become the cauldron in which the family's personality is produced. These accounts of beating misfortune, whether individual, cultural, or financial, become basic to the family's personality, molding their reaction to difficulties and affliction in the present.
   In the retelling of these stories, there arises an aggregate memory — a repository of solidarity drawn upon in the midst of hardship. The narratives of difficulty are not related with a feeling of exploitation but rather with a flexibility that addresses the unyielding soul of

the family. It is inside these accounts that the seeds of aggregate strength are planted, as every age gains from the victories and hardships of the past.

The family's ancestry is likewise an embroidery woven with the brilliant strings of adoration. Love that rises above the limits of time, associating grandparents to grandkids, and guardians to kids. An adoration perseveres through the times of bliss and endures the hardships of difficulties. This persevering through adoration turns into an inheritance went down through the ages, making a familial bond that is both delicate and strong.

Installed inside the family's ancestry are likewise the reverberations of shared values. Whether it be a guarantee to genuineness, a respect for difficult work, or a commitment to local area administration, these qualities are the paste that ties the family together. The common qualities structure the establishment whereupon the family's aggregate personality rests, forming their choices, activities, and communications with the world.

The family's ancestry, nonetheless, is definitely not a static remnant of the past; a powerful power shapes the present and illuminates what's to come. Every age contributes its own part to the continuous account, adding layers of intricacy and wealth to the family story. The practices, customs, and values that have been passed down are not fossilized relics but rather living practices that develop and adjust to the evolving times.

In investigating the family's ancestry, we experience the interconnected trap of connections that structure the core of their aggregate presence. The connections between kin, the ties that tight spot guardians and kids, and the associations with more distant family individuals make a complex yet amicable organization of connections. These connections are not resistant to difficulties, conflicts, or false impressions, but rather it is inside the pot of these elements that the family finds the genuine importance of solidarity.

Past the singular stories, the family's ancestry is set apart by shared achievements and aggregate accomplishments. Whether it be instructive achievements, proficient victories, or local area commitments, these common victories become markers of the family's excursion. Festivities are not lone occasions but rather public articulations of satisfaction, mirroring the interconnectedness of the relatives.

The qualities went down through the ages are a wellspring of solidarity as well as a wellspring of direction. They act as a compass that assists the family with exploring the intricacies of the cutting edge world while remaining consistent with their center standards. In a world set apart by fast change and moving social standards, the family's qualities become an anchor, giving dependability and a feeling of rootedness.

As we set out on this excursion through the chronicles of time, the family's ancestry unfurls like an esteemed novel — a story loaded up with stories of adoration, flexibility, shared values, and aggregate strength. A set of experiences rises above individual encounters, winding around an embroidery that ties the family together in a rich mosaic of personality and having a place. In the parts that follow, we will dive further into the lived encounters, customs, difficulties, and festivities that characterize the present and shape the eventual fate of this uncommon family — a family whose roots run profound, securing them in a tradition of solidarity and shared euphoria.

2. **Emphasis on the significance of unity and collective strength.**

At the core of Congruity Property lies a significant accentuation on solidarity — a power that ties the family in a mind boggling dance of shared encounters and aggregate strength. This accentuation is certainly not a simple dynamic ideal however a no nonsense way of thinking that shapes the actual texture of the family's presence. Solidarity, in its heap structures, turns into the foundation whereupon the family constructs its establishment, encouraging a feeling of harmony that rises above the limits of distinction.

The meaning of solidarity inside Amicability Residence isn't bound to the actual spaces shared by its individuals. It stretches out past the walls of the home, penetrating the very air the family relaxes. This accentuation on solidarity is an acknowledgment that the strength of the family lies in its aggregate soul — a joined embroidery of hearts, brains, and spirits.

It is inside this solidarity that the family finds flexibility, support, and a mutual perspective that hoists their aggregate process.

The common spaces inside Congruity Estate become a material whereupon the craft of solidarity is painted. From the collective kitchen where recipes are shared and culinary stories are turned to the front room where giggling reverberations through shared stories, each side of the home turns into a demonstration of the family's obligation to fellowship. It is in these common spaces that the unremarkable becomes uncommon, as everyday schedules change into ceremonies of association and holding.

The accentuation on solidarity isn't a call for consistency; rather, an affirmation of the excellence emerges from the variety of individual qualities and viewpoints. Concordance Property blossoms with the possibility that solidarity doesn't mean the deletion of individual personalities however, all things being equal, the agreeable incorporation of these remarkable characteristics into a firm entirety. Every relative is a fundamental note in the orchestra of solidarity, adding to the tune of shared encounters.

In the midst of festivity, the meaning of solidarity turns out to be considerably more articulated. Whether it be birthday events, occasions, or exceptional accomplishments, the family meets up in a cheerful melody of shared bliss. These snapshots of festivity act as tokens of the aggregate bliss that arises when people join out of a sense of kinship. It is at these times that the genuine strength of the family sparkles, as the delight isn't divided yet shared, amplified by the solidarity of hearts cheering as one.

Nonetheless, the accentuation on solidarity isn't a safeguard against the difficulties that life unavoidably presents. All things considered, it turns into a wellspring of versatility, a solid support point that upholds the family through the tempests of difficulty. When confronted with hardships, the family draws strength from its aggregate soul, changing difficulties into open doors for development and fortitude. At these times, the meaning of solidarity isn't simply a philosophical ideal; it is a lived insight, a life saver that keeps the family secured in fierce times.

The solidarity inside Concordance Estate is definitely not a static substance; a unique power develops with the changing tides of life. As relatives develop, mature, and face the moving scenes of their singular processes, the accentuation on solidarity turns into a core value that adjusts to the rhythmic movement of time. It is a promise to remaining associated, even as the flows of life pull people this way and that.

The meaning of solidarity is woven into the very customs that characterize Congruity Estate. Whether it be the yearly family gathering that unites family members from all over or the week by week family meals that act as anchors in the mood of life, these practices become customs of solidarity. They are minutes when the family deliberately meets up, building up the securities that tie them in a common embroidery of adoration, understanding, and shared help.

Solidarity isn't simply an idea inside Congruity Property; a lived reality impacts direction, critical thinking, and how clashes are explored. When confronted with choices that influence the family, there is an aggregate pondering — an acknowledgment that each voice is vital for the concordance of the entirety. Clashes, when they emerge, are drawn nearer not as fights to be won but rather as any open doors for grasping, split the difference, and the reinforcing of the familial bond.

The meaning of solidarity isn't restricted to the present; it reaches out into the inheritance that Congruity Property tries to leave for people in the future. The family perceives that the upsides of fellowship and aggregate strength are gifts to be passed down — a legacy that rises above material riches. The accentuation on solidarity turns into a signal directing the family as they explore the sensitive harmony between saving practices and embracing the development of the familial story.

In the bigger setting of the world, the accentuation on solidarity inside Congruity Residence turns into a microcosm of the cultural concordance that is frequently looked for yet some of the time slippery. It is a demonstration of the possibility that, inside the limits of a home, solidarity can be a strong power for positive change. The family perceives that their aggregate strength can possibly swell past their walls, impacting the networks they draw in with and adding to the more extensive embroidered artwork of human association.

As we peer into the profundities of Concordance Estate, obviously the meaning of solidarity is definitely not a grand ideal however a core value that shapes the family's personality, choices, and encounters. It is an affirmation that, in solidarity, the family tracks down strength, satisfaction, and a mutual perspective that changes the customary into the exceptional. In the sections that follow, we will dive further into the lived encounters, customs, difficulties, and festivities that emerge from this accentuation on solidarity — a power that meshes the family's story into a rich embroidery of interconnected lives.

3. Narration of how the family's roots shape their strong bond.

In the embroidery of Congruity Residence, the underlying foundations of the family run profound, mooring every part in a common history that shapes the actual quintessence of their solid bond. The portrayal of these roots is an excursion through time, following the strides of predecessors whose accounts reverberation through the passageways of the present. It is an acknowledgment that the family's personality is definitely not a disengaged preview however a continuum, with every age adding a layer to the story of aggregate strength and persevering through association.

The familial roots find their starting point in the stories passed down from one age to another. These stories are more than verifiable records;

they are the soul that courses through the family's veins, interfacing them to a genealogy of strength, love, and shared values.

It is inside these accounts that the seeds of the family's solid bond are planted, as every part learns of the victories and afflictions of the people who preceded.

The family's foundations are frequently entwined with a particular geographic area — a spot that becomes sacrosanct in the narrating of familial history. Whether it be the tribal home, a town, or a town, this geographic anchor fills in as an establishing force, giving a feeling of progression and having a place. The actual spaces related with the family's underlying foundations become something beyond areas; they are archives of memory, imbued with the giggling, tears, and shared encounters of previous eras.

The excursion through the foundations of Concordance Residence is a journey to tribal grounds, a reconnection with the spots that have seen the unfurling show of family ancestry. A stroll through the scenes formed the qualities, customs, and aggregate character of the family. The relatives, whether genuinely present or through the retelling of stories, become connected to these spots, making a feeling of rootedness that rises above existence.

As the portrayal unfurls, it becomes obvious that the underlying foundations of Agreement Property are grounded set up as well as in the qualities gave over through the ages. The ethos of difficult work, uprightness, sympathy, and a guarantee to family turns into a brilliant string that winds through the family's story. These qualities are not relics of the past; they are living rules that guide the family in their everyday associations, choices, and connections.

The family's foundations are much of the time set apart by huge achievements — minutes that become standards in the story of their common history. Whether it be the relocation of progenitors looking for a superior life, the foundation of a privately-run company, or the defeating of misfortunes, these achievements become sections in the aggregate story. It is in the comprehension of these crucial minutes that the relatives find the strength that emerges from a tradition of flexibility and assurance.

Generational photos, protected in collections and casings, become visual demonstrations of the progression of time and the congruity of family ties. The countenances in sepia-conditioned or variety pictures might change, however the familial similarity and the common grins address a typical heredity. Each photo is a frozen second in the stream of time, catching the embodiment of family bonds and the intergenerational string that interfaces the past to the present.

The underlying foundations of Congruity Estate additionally reach out to the social and ethnic embroidery from which the family arose. Social practices, language, and customs are not curios of a past time but rather living articulations that shape the family's personality. Whether it be the festival of social celebrations, the planning of customary dishes, or the recognition of ceremonies, these social roots act as extensions interfacing the family to a more extensive legacy.

In the portrayal of the family's foundations, there is an acknowledgment that not all accounts are stories of outright achievement. The roots may likewise contain accounts of difficulty, penance, and flexibility even with misfortune. These accounts, however pervaded with difficulties, become wellsprings of motivation, representing the determination and backbone expected to face the hardships of life. It is in the affirmation of the two victories and battles that the relatives find a more profound comprehension of their underlying foundations and the bonds that join them.

The family's foundations, while molding an aggregate personality, likewise perceive the singular stories that add to the mosaic of the entirety. Every part conveys a novel story — an individual excursion that meets with the more extensive familial history. It is inside the embroidery of individual stories that the wealth of the family's aggregate experience is uncovered, as every part turns into a narrator by their own doing.

As the portrayal unfurls, the family's underlying foundations become a wellspring of motivation, a wellspring of insight from which the current age draws strength. The difficulties looked by progenitors become accounts of affliction as well as stories of strength and win. It is in the comprehension of these roots that the relatives find a common heritage — an inheritance that stretches out past material abundance to the immaterial fortunes of affection, solidarity, and a typical reason.

The foundations of Congruity Property are not relics consigned to the past; they are living substances that keep on affecting the family's present and future. The portrayal is definitely not a static memory of verifiable occasions; it is a unique investigation of how the family's foundations shape their reactions to the difficulties and chances of the contemporary world. The examples gained from hereditary stories become core values, offering a compass that coordinates the family through the intricacies of the cutting edge age.

In the hug of their underlying foundations, the family tracks down a wellspring of solidness and congruity — a tie that associates them to an option that could be bigger than themselves. The portrayal of these roots is definitely not a nostalgic longing for quite a long time passed by; it is a festival of the versatility, love, and shared values that have been gone down through the ages. It is an acknowledgment that the family's solid security isn't an incident however a conscious result of the narratives, encounters, and values that structure the bedrock of Concordance Estate.

The portrayal of the family's foundations is an excursion through existence, investigating the scenes, achievements, values, and social embroideries that have formed Congruity Estate. It is an acknowledgment that the family's story isn't bound to the present however is a continuum that stretches out into the past and ventures forward into what's to come. The roots, profoundly implanted in the familial story, act as anchors that ground the family in a tradition of association, versatility, and persevering through strength.

Chapter 1

"The Shared Space"

The Common Space is a multi-layered idea that reaches out past the actual domain, rising above the simple limits of design or topography. It is a powerful interchange of thoughts, feelings, and communications that mix to shape a climate where people meet up to share encounters, encourage associations, and make a feeling of public character. This common space isn't bound to a particular district; it envelops both unmistakable and elusive components, winding around an embroidery that mirrors the shared perspective of the people who possess it.

At its center, the common space is an impression of the principal human requirement for association and having a place. It is where people settle on something worth agreeing on, rising above contrasts in foundation, culture, or convictions. In actual terms, shared spaces can appear as common social occasion regions, parks, courts, or even the common spaces inside a home. Nonetheless, the substance of the common space reaches out past the substantial designs; it dwells in the common minutes, shared stories, and shared desires that tight spot individuals together.

One of the principal qualities of the common space is its ability to encourage coordinated effort and participation. Inside such a space, people bring their one of a kind viewpoints, gifts, and abilities to the aggregate table.

Whether in a working environment, a public venue, or a web-based gathering, the common space turns into a favorable place for development and imagination. The trading of thoughts and the cooperative energy that rises up out of different commitments hoist the common space into a domain where the entire is genuinely more prominent than the amount of its parts.

Moreover, the common space is a demonstration of the vote based soul inborn in human social orders. It is a space where voices are heard, suppositions are esteemed, and choices are made all things considered. This majority rule ethos isn't restricted to formal administration structures; it saturates regular connections inside the common space. It is where inclusivity rules, where people feel engaged to take part in molding the climate they altogether possess.

In a more extensive cultural setting, shared spaces assume an essential part in molding the social personality of networks. Public squares, social focuses, and common tourist spots become the materials whereupon the stories of a general public unfurl. These spaces become an impression of shared narratives, shared esteems, and shared yearnings. Through open workmanship, festivities, and widespread developments, the common space turns into a living document of the aggregate memory of a local area, cultivating a feeling of progression and connectedness across ages.

Innovation, in its different structures, has additionally reclassified the idea of shared space. Virtual stages, web-based entertainment, and online networks have broadened the limits of actual shared spaces to the advanced domain. The interconnectedness worked with by innovation has empowered people to share their lives, thoughts, and encounters on a worldwide scale. The common space in the advanced age is described by moment network, permitting individuals to frame networks and offer information regardless of geological distances.

In any case, the idea of the common space isn't without its difficulties. As social orders become progressively different, exploring the intricacies of shared spaces requires a guarantee to inclusivity and regard for contrasts. The common space, whether physical or computerized, should be where variety isn't only endured however celebrated. It requires deliberate endeavors to establish conditions where people from fluctuated foundations feel appreciated, heard, and esteemed.

The common space is a multi-layered and dynamic idea that goes past the actual designs that characterize it. It is a sign of the human requirement for association, joint effort, and having a place. Whether in actual networks or advanced domains, shared spaces are the pots where connections are manufactured, thoughts are hatched, and aggregate personalities are formed. Sustaining and protecting the quintessence of the common space is fundamental for building versatile, comprehensive, and energetic networks that endure for an extremely long period.

1.1 Exploration of the physical and emotional aspects of the family home.

The family home, an actual construction saturated with profound reverberation, fills in as a sanctuary where the unpredictable embroidery of human connections is woven. To leave on an investigation of the family home is to dig into the blend of unmistakable spaces and immaterial feelings that characterize the forms of familial bonds. This investigation envelops the engineering, plan, and usefulness of the residence, while simultaneously digging into the nuanced profound scenes that penetrate the walls.

In its actual sign, the family home is a design encapsulation of haven and security, giving an unmistakable shelter to its occupants. The plan of the home, from its format to its stylish components, adds to the general mood and usefulness. Contemplations of spatial game plans, like shared living spaces, confidential quarters, and mutual regions, shape the elements of family communications. The actual design of the home impacts the progression of day to day existence, influencing the recurrence and nature of familial commitment.

Engineering components, like the selection of materials, varieties, and goods, add to the tactile experience inside the family home. The glow of wooden floors, the delicateness of very much worn couches, and the shades of the walls all assume a part in establishing a climate that resounds with the lived encounters of the family. The actual parts of the home become vessels of memory, taking the stand concerning the progression of time and the advancement of familial elements.

However, past the blocks and mortar, the family home rises above its rawness to turn into a profound asylum. Feelings, similar to elusive strings, wind through the spaces, making an extraordinary close to home mark that characterizes the pith of the nuclear family. The profound parts of the family home are well established in the common encounters, customs, and achievements that unfurl inside its limits. It is a vault of giggling, tears, festivities, and commonplace schedules that add to the close to home embroidery of familial life.

The family home fills in as the setting for the unfurling show of day to day presence, where the recurring pattern of feelings are entwined with the everyday and the uncommon. From the cheerful reverberations of youngsters playing to the quieted discussions between guardians, the home turns into a residing material whereupon the profound story of the family is painted. It is a space where love is communicated through shared feasts, support is presented in the midst of pain, and a feeling of having a place is developed through shared customs.

The profound parts of the family home are likewise profoundly associated with the idea of wellbeing and security. Inside its walls, people track down comfort and a feeling of shelter from the difficulties of the outer world.

The profound security given by the family home makes an establishment for self-awareness and investigation. It is inside this protected climate that people feel engaged to face challenges, express weaknesses, and manufacture their personalities.

Besides, the family home is a vessel for the intergenerational transmission of values, customs, and social legacy. It is a storehouse of stories, tales, and familial legend that ties ages together. The walls of the family home reverberation with the voices of progenitors and the reverberation of shared narratives. This transmission of social and profound heritages makes a feeling of progression and having a place, cultivating an association with the past that improves the present.

Be that as it may, the profound scene of the family home isn't generally one of immaculate concordance. It is a landscape set apart by the intricacies of human connections, where clashes, pressures, and difficulties likewise track down articulation. The profound elements inside the family home can be both sustaining and requesting, mirroring the complex snare of human feelings. Battles for independence, conflicts of characters, and the discussion of limits are innate parts of familial life that add to the profound surface of the home.

In the midst of conflict, the family home turns into a cauldron for profound strength and development. It is inside this personal setting that people figure out how to explore the complexities of compromise, sympathy, and split the difference. The personal difficulties experienced inside the family home add to the advancement of the capacity to appreciate people on a profound level and relational abilities, getting ready people for the intricacies of the more extensive social world.

Moreover, the family home is an observer to the recurrent idea of life, from the richness of experience growing up to the intelligent snapshots of advanced age. A space develops close by the family, reflecting the changes and changes that portray the various phases of life. The profound parts of the family home are interlaced with the evolving needs, yearnings, and elements of its occupants.

The family home, as a locus of both physical and profound importance, is a unique space where the crossing point of design and feelings shapes the establishment for the unpredictable dance of familial connections. To additionally disentangle the diverse idea of the family home, it is basic to investigate its job in molding individual characters, cultivating socialization, and giving a material to the declaration of social qualities.

At its center, the family home assumes a vital part in the development and forming of individual characters. It is inside the walls of the home that kids make their most memorable strides, utter their most memorable words, and manufacture the underlying groundworks of their healthy identity.

The actual spaces inside the home, like rooms and individual corners, become asylums for reflection and self-disclosure. These spaces act as confidential areas where people, particularly teenagers, arrange their advancing personalities from the look of the outer world.

The familial climate, with its complicated snare of connections, impacts the advancement of individual qualities, convictions, and perspectives. It is through everyday collaborations with relatives that people incorporate social standards, moral standards, and social assumptions. The family home, as a microcosm of society, turns into the underlying preparation ground where people get familiar with the complexities of human connections, compassion, and participation. Along these lines, the profound scene of the family home contributes altogether to the development of social and moral compasses that guide people in their more extensive cooperations with the world.

Besides, the family home fills in as a pot for the socialization of its individuals. It is a space where people become familiar with the specialty of correspondence, discussion, and compromise. Shared living spaces become fields for the exchange of individual limits and the advancement of relational abilities. These social elements inside the family home are instrumental in planning people for their jobs as friendly creatures in the more extensive cultural setting.

The family home, as a setting for day to day schedules and customs, gives a structure to the foundation of shared customs and values. From family dinners to special festivals, these customs add to a feeling of progression and shared personality. The close to home reverberation of these practices makes enduring recollections, shaping the reason for an aggregate familial culture that ties ages together. Through these common ceremonies, the family home turns into a social anchor, communicating the rich embroidery of legacy and values starting with one age then onto the next.

In any case, the family home is certainly not a static substance yet a developing space that adjusts to the changing requirements and elements of its occupants. As kids develop, venture out from home, and possibly get back with their own families, the family home turns into an observer to the repetitive idea of life. The profound forms of the home shift with every life stage, from the abundance of youth to the pensive snapshots of advanced age. It is inside this powerful climate that familial bonds are tried and reinforced, adding to the strength and versatility of the nuclear family.

However, the profound parts of the family home are not safe to outside impacts and cultural changes. Financial tensions, social movements, and worldwide elements can apply significant consequences for the profound environment inside the home. The family home turns into an intelligent surface that reflects the difficulties and vulnerabilities of the outer world. In the midst of emergency, the profound strength got from familial bonds can act as a wellspring of flexibility, offering comfort and backing to its individuals.

The profound scene of the family home is likewise unpredictably associated with the idea of home as a place of refuge. It is inside these walls that people look for shelter from the stressors and requests of the outer world. The profound security given by the family home cultivates a feeling of having a place, acknowledgment, and unrestricted love. It is a safe-haven where people can uncover their weaknesses, express their feelings, and track down comfort in the soothing hug of familial ties.

Nonetheless, the profound security of the family home isn't uniform across all families. Financial abberations, social contrasts, and individual conditions can add to fluctuated close to home encounters inside various nuclear families. While certain people might find resolute help and profound security inside their familial surroundings, others might wrestle with difficulties and vulnerabilities that influence their close to home prosperity.

The investigation of the family home uncovers a nuanced transaction between its physical and profound aspects. It is a space where design and feelings merge to shape individual characters, encourage socialization, and give a material to the declaration of social qualities. The family home, with its consistently developing close to home scene, is a demonstration of the strength of familial bonds and the significant effect of shared encounters on the human excursion. As people explore the actual spaces and profound intricacies of their family homes, they add to the continuous story of the human experience inside the safe-haven of familial connections.

1.2 Descriptions of shared spaces and how they foster togetherness.

Shared spaces, both physical and figurative, hold a significant importance in the embroidery of human communication, establishing conditions where people meet up, cultivating fellowship, and building a feeling of local area. These spaces rise above simple topographical areas; they include mutual regions, virtual stages, and divided encounters that span the holes among people, sustaining associations and shared personalities.

In the actual domain, public social affair regions like parks, courts, and public venues stand as substantial encapsulations of shared spaces that work with harmony. These spaces are intended to be comprehensive, welcoming individuals from assorted foundations to join, cooperate, and participate in aggregate exercises. The engineering and format of these actual common spaces assume a critical part in empowering socialization, with open plans, happy with seating, and intelligent elements making an environment helpful for significant associations.

Consider a clamoring local area park, for example, where individuals of any age accumulate for relaxation, exercise, and mingling. The green fields, jungle gyms, and seating regions give a material to unconstrained connections, encouraging a feeling of having a place among inhabitants.

Shared actual spaces like these become center points for the trading of thoughts, social articulation, and the producing of kinships, separating the obstructions that frequently portray current metropolitan living.

In the computerized age, virtual shared spaces have arisen as strong facilitators of harmony. Online people group, virtual entertainment stages, and cooperative spaces rethink the idea of shared spaces, empowering people to interface across geological distances. These virtual domains act as discussions for the trading of thoughts, support, and shared encounters, rising above actual restrictions to make a feeling of local area.

For instance, online discussions committed to explicit interests, leisure activities, or care groups unite similar people who may very well never have run into each other in the actual world. The common space in the computerized domain turns into a stage for the development of virtual networks, where individuals can share experiences, look for counsel, and celebrate normal interests. The feeling of fellowship developed in these web-based spaces delineates the groundbreaking force of shared encounters, even without any actual vicinity.

The working environment, as one more type of shared space, assumes a critical part in encouraging harmony among partners. Office conditions with open designs, collective regions, and cooperative work areas set out open doors for unconstrained connections and collaboration. The common space of the work environment turns into a pot for thought age, cooperation, and the development of an aggregate ethos.

Notwithstanding actual closeness, the working environment shared space frequently includes shared objectives, values, and an aggregate feeling of direction. Group gatherings, meetings to generate new ideas, and cooperative undertakings add to the production of a firm work culture. The common space inside the working environment works with proficient cooperation as well as sustains a feeling of kinship and shared help among partners.

Past physical and virtual spaces, shared encounters structure a vital part of harmony. Occasions, festivities, and ceremonies become shared spaces in time, giving open doors to people to meet up, bond, and make enduring recollections. Consider a social celebration where individuals assemble to celebrate shared customs, or a family supper where ages meet up to share a dinner. These common transient spaces add to a feeling of coherence, cultivating associations across time and ages.

The common experience of misfortune can likewise make strong shared spaces, fashioning profound bonds among people confronting normal difficulties. Whether it's a local area meeting up in the result of a cataclysmic event or a care group for people managing comparative difficulties, shared spaces conceived out of shared battles embody the flexibility and strength that rise out of aggregate fellowship.

To comprehend the effect of shared spaces on harmony, investigating the mental and humanistic aspects at play is fundamental. Shared spaces give a feeling of having a place, tending to an essential human requirement for association and local area. The simple presence of others in a common space makes a social setting that impacts conduct, cultivating a feeling of responsibility, sympathy, and shared understanding.

Social clinicians accentuate the idea of social assistance, wherein the presence of others upgrades individual execution and inspiration. In shared spaces, whether physical or virtual, the familiarity with being essential for a bigger aggregate can motivate people to contribute, team up, and connect all the more effectively. The common space turns into an impetus for positive social elements, empowering people to rise above individual interests and line up with the aggregate great.

Besides, shared spaces add to the development of social character — a feeling of having a place with a specific gathering or local area. This common personality, whether established in topographical closeness, normal interests, or shared encounters, makes a feeling of "us" against "them," encouraging a shared mindset. The common space turns into an emblematic portrayal of this social personality, supporting a common feeling of direction, standards, and values.

The job of shared spaces in alleviating social detachment and depression is especially vital. In a period where mechanical progressions strangely work with network and disengagement all the while, shared physical and virtual spaces become cures to the estrangement that can go with present day residing. Old consideration habitats, public venues, and online care groups all capability as shared spaces that give roads to social communication, diminishing sensations of disconnection and cultivating a feeling of local area.

With regards to metropolitan preparation, the idea of placemaking underlines the purposeful production of shared spaces that upgrade the personal satisfaction and fortify social bonds. Very much planned public spaces, like passerby cordial roads, dynamic business sectors, and social center points, add to the imperativeness of a local area. These common spaces become central focuses for social collaborations, social trade, and local area commitment, cultivating a feeling of satisfaction and personality among occupants.

To genuinely see the value in the effect of shared spaces on fellowship, it is fundamental to recognize the likely difficulties and contemplations related with these conditions. Shared spaces, whether physical or virtual, can become fields where social imbalances and prohibitions are propagated. In metropolitan settings, for instance, improvement and inconsistent admittance to public spaces can bring about the underestimation of specific gatherings, thwarting the inclusivity that common spaces in a perfect world address.

Likewise, virtual shared spaces can at times build up existing social progressive systems or protected, closed off areas, restricting openness to assorted viewpoints. It is urgent to perceive and address these difficulties to guarantee that common spaces really mirror the variety and extravagance of human encounters. Deliberate endeavors to advance inclusivity, availability, and variety inside shared spaces are fundamental for establishing conditions that really encourage harmony.

To dig further into the investigation of shared spaces and their groundbreaking impact on fellowship, it is basic to consider the social, monetary, and verifiable aspects that shape these conditions. Shared spaces, both physical and virtual, are not uniform substances but rather are rather unpredictably weaved with the social texture of explicit networks and social orders.

Socially, shared spaces frequently act as impressions of cultural qualities, standards, and ceremonies. Public squares, strict spaces, and collective social event regions become fields where social articulation and personality are exhibited. Consider a clamoring market square where craftsmans show their specialties, performers share their tunes, and local people participate in energetic discussions. These common spaces become performance centers for the social embroidery of a local area, encouraging a feeling of shared legacy and supporting the bonds that integrate people.

Widespread developments and celebrations further highlight the job of shared spaces in the festival of variety and the assertion of aggregate character. Whether it's a festival in Rio de Janeiro, a Diwali festivity in India, or a conventional function in an African town, these common spaces become stages for the statement of social pride. The fellowship experienced during these occasions rises above individual contrasts, making a feeling of solidarity that is well established in shared customs and social stories.

Monetarily, shared spaces add to the essentialness and flexibility of neighborhood networks. Markets, town squares, and collective spaces act as financial center points where exchange, business venture, and monetary trades thrive. These common spaces give valuable open doors to independent companies to flourish, cultivating a feeling of financial reliance among local area individuals. The monetary imperativeness of shared spaces contributes not exclusively to the monetary prosperity of people yet in addition to the general success of the local area.

By and large, shared spaces have been fields where social developments, transformations, and crucial crossroads in history have unfurled. Public squares, roads, and get-together regions become emblematic stages for aggregate activity and the statement of cultural change. Consider notorious minutes like the social liberties walks on Washington, D.C's. Public Shopping center or the fights at Tahrir Square during the Bedouin Spring. These common spaces become carved in the authentic memory of social orders, addressing the force of fellowship in rocking the boat and supporting for extraordinary change.

Nonetheless, the verifiable aspect additionally highlights the challenged idea of shared spaces. Many shared spaces, particularly in metropolitan conditions, bear the characteristics of verifiable disparities, segregation, and power awkward nature. Parks, roads, and public offices might be named after verifiable figures whose heritages are related with mistreatment or imperialism. The change of shared spaces requires a basic assessment of these verifiable stories and deliberate endeavors to establish conditions that recognize and address verifiable treacheries.

In the computerized period, the idea of shared virtual spaces has arisen as an extraordinary power in molding worldwide fellowship. Online stages, web-based entertainment organizations, and virtual networks have reclassified the limits of shared spaces, rising above topographical constraints. People from different foundations can now associate, share encounters, and fabricate networks in computerized domains. The common space in the virtual world turns into a fairly open field where voices, thoughts, and societies blend.

Computerized shared spaces likewise assume an essential part in enhancing underrepresented voices and encouraging worldwide discussions. Virtual entertainment developments, hashtag activism, and online support crusades become shared spaces where people join around normal causes. The computerized domain turns into a useful asset for democratizing data and making virtual networks that rise above geological, social, and financial limits.

In any case, the advanced common space isn't without its difficulties. The peculiarity of online closed quarters, where people are presented to data and points of view that line up with their current convictions, can thwart authentic discourse and understanding. Exploring computerized shared spaces requires a nuanced way to deal with guarantee that these conditions encourage inclusivity, variety, and significant collaborations.

To investigate the effect of shared spaces on harmony, recognizing the job of plan and deliberate planning is likewise fundamental. Metropolitan organizers, planners, and local area pioneers assume urgent parts in forming actual shared spaces. Plan components that advance openness, inclusivity, and social responsiveness are fundamental for establishing conditions that really encourage harmony. Public craftsmanship, green spaces, and guest plans add to the general feeling of shared spaces, empowering associations and local area commitment.

Similarly significant is the thought of how shared spaces can resolve issues of supportability and natural cognizance. Eco-accommodating plan standards, sustainable power sources, and the fuse of nature into shared spaces contribute not exclusively to the prosperity of people yet in addition to the more extensive environmental wellbeing of networks. Shared spaces, when planned in view of supportability, become models for capable metropolitan turn of events and ecological stewardship.

Also, the deliberate preparation of shared spaces includes local area commitment and participatory cycles. Occupants, as key partners, ought to have a voice in forming the plan and motivation behind shared spaces inside their networks. This cooperative methodology guarantees that common spaces truly mirror the necessities, desires, and social subtleties of the people who possess them.

In the domain of work environment shared spaces, the idea of the workplace as a cooperative and imaginative climate has acquired unmistakable quality. Shared work areas, adaptable office plans, and co-operative regions are made to advance innovativeness, collaboration, and representative prosperity. These common spaces rise above conventional office designs, offering dynamic conditions that take special care of the different requirements and workstyles of current experts.

The purposeful plan of work environment shared spaces likewise reaches out to contemplations of representative prosperity, wellbeing, and balance between serious and fun activities. Collective regions that cultivate unwinding, socialization, and mental revival add to a positive working environment culture. Shared spaces inside the work environment become centers for thought age, information trade, and the development of a feeling of having a place among partners.

Be that as it may, the continuous pattern of remote work and virtual co-ordinated effort presents difficulties to the customary idea of the working environment shared space. As additional people embrace adaptable work game plans, the meaning of shared work areas develops to incorporate virtual gathering stages, cooperative programming, and advanced project the board instruments. The test lies in keeping a feeling of harmony and group union in a computerized scene, underlining the requirement for deliberate procedures that rise above actual limits.

The investigation of shared spaces and their job in encouraging fellowship envelops a rich embroidery of social, monetary, verifiable, and configuration aspects. Whether physical or virtual, shared spaces are dynamic conditions where people join, communicate, and fabricate associations that rise above individual limits. From the lively market squares that reverberation with social variety to the advanced discussions that join voices across landmasses, shared spaces embody the significant effect of harmony on the human experience. As social orders explore the intricacies of shared spaces, the purposeful development of comprehensive, open, and reasonable conditions turns into an aggregate undertaking, molding the story of harmony for a long time into the future.

1.3 Anecdotes illustrating the importance of a common environment.

Tales, similar to light emissions, have the ability to enlighten the significance of a typical climate, exhibiting the significant effect that common spaces have on people, connections, and networks.

These accounts, woven into the texture of regular daily existence, epitomize the groundbreaking impact of conditions where individuals meet up, cultivating a feeling of association, solidarity, and shared character.

Consider the clamoring neighborhood bistro, where the fragrant mix of newly ground beans blends with the murmur of discussion. In this mutual sanctuary, various people end up attracted to a typical space. It is here that regulars and newbies the same find a common love for the rich fragrance of espresso and the consoling vibe of a recognizable setting. Through the straightforward demonstration of tasting some espresso, outsiders become neighbors, framing associations that reach out past the limits of the bistro.

In such conditions, a shared belief arises, making a space for unconstrained communications and shared minutes. Take, for example, the tale of two people who, in spite of being outsiders, end up participated in a discussion over a common appreciation for a nearby craftsman's work showed on the bistro's walls. In that normal climate, craftsmanship turns into an extension, interfacing different lives and cultivating a feeling of fellowship through the common experience of stylish appreciation.

These common spaces become observers to the sections of individual and aggregate stories. In a local park, guardians assemble consistently to watch their kids play. In the midst of the chuckling, scratched knees, and extemporaneous soccer coordinates, a feeling of local area blooms. The recreation area, with its open green spaces and jungle gym gear, turns into a material for the common encounters of being a parent. The significance of this normal climate lies not simply in the actual space it accommodates diversion yet in the bonds that structure among guardians, making a steady organization that reaches out past playdates.

Shared spaces stretch out past the nearby and recognizable, rising above geological limits to become worldwide gathering grounds. Consider the story of an explorer investigating a clamoring lodging familiar room. Here, voyagers from different corners of the world join, each with an interesting story to tell. In this transient yet mutual climate, fellowships are produced over shared travel stories, social trades, and the energy of investigation. The lodging well known room changes into a microcosm of worldwide fellowship, stressing the shared characteristic of human encounters regardless of different foundations.

The working environment, a quintessential common climate, is a cauldron for joint effort and shared accomplishments. In the tale of a startup's modest starting points, a little office space fills in as the scenery for imaginative meetings to generate new ideas, late-evening coding long distance races, and the common victories and difficulties of developing something from the beginning. The fellowship inside the common work area turns into the main thrust behind the organization's prosperity, showing the way in which a typical climate can catalyze development, collaboration, and an aggregate feeling of direction.

However, shared conditions are not invulnerable to snapshots of contention and pressure. In the story of a local area garden, neighbors meet up to develop a common space of vegetation and peacefulness. Nonetheless, conflicts surface over establishing decisions, watering plans, and the utilization of public devices. In exploring these difficulties, the local area learns the significance of open correspondence, split the difference, and the aggregate liability that accompanies sharing a typical climate. The nursery turns into a similitude for the sensitive equilibrium expected in keeping up with fellowship in the midst of variety.

In the computerized age, the virtual world turns into a common space where associations are fashioned past actual limitations. Virtual entertainment stages, discussions, and online networks become settings for different accounts to unfurl. Consider the narrative of a singular finding comfort in a web-based help bunch during testing times. In this virtual safe-haven, people from various corners of the globe share their battles, offer support, and structure associations in light of shared encounters. The significance of the normal computerized climate lies in its ability to give a feeling of having a place and backing, rising above geological distances.

Shared spaces likewise assume a significant part in the training scene. In the record of a school library, understudies from different disciplines join to review, research, and team up. The library, with its quiet understanding corridors and public review tables, turns into a common climate that works with scholastic trade and the cross-fertilization of thoughts. Here, information turns into a typical money, and the library changes into a space where different scholarly pursuits meet.

The meaning of shared spaces turns out to be much more articulated in multicultural settings. In a multicultural area, people from various ethnic foundations share collective spaces like neighborhood markets and widespread developments. A story unfurls where neighbors celebrate assorted celebrations, share conventional cooking styles, and take part in social trade programs. The common spaces become conductors for shared figuring out, encouraging appreciation for social variety and improving the aggregate embroidered artwork of the local area.

With regards to everyday life, the actual home turns into a quintessential common climate. Think about a family's kitchen, where ages meet up to get ready dinners, share stories, and pass down culinary customs. In this recognizable space, the clack of pots and container turns into a soundtrack to shared encounters, making a bond that stretches out past blood relations. The kitchen embodies how a typical climate sustains familial fellowship and turns into a store of shared recollections.

The story of a local area driven drive embodies the groundbreaking force of shared spaces in making positive social change. In a weather beaten metropolitan area, occupants choose to recover a disregarded park and change it into a lively local area space. The common work to renew the recreation area turns into an impetus for more extensive local area commitment, lighting a deep satisfaction and proprietorship among inhabitants.

The recreation area, when an image of disregard, turns into a demonstration of the groundbreaking effect of a common climate on the prosperity of a local area.

In pondering these tales, a consistent idea arises — the common spaces, whether physical or virtual, act as cauldrons for human association, understanding, and joint effort. From the local bistro to the worldwide web-based local area, these conditions set out open doors for people to rise above uniqueness and partake in an option that could be more significant than themselves. The significance of a typical climate lies in its actual qualities as well as in the elusive components that develop a feeling of having a place, common perspective, and aggregate personality.

These stories additionally highlight the nuanced idea of shared spaces, recognizing that they are not idealistic domains resistant to challenges.

Clashes, conflicts, and snapshots of strain are woven into the stories, uncovering that the strength of harmony lies in the capacity to altogether explore and beat these difficulties. The common climate turns into a research facility for the development of strength, compassion, and the comprehension that fellowship is a dynamic and developing excursion.

Besides, the job of deliberate plan, comprehensive preparation, and local area commitment inside shared spaces arises as a common topic. These accounts show that the intentional creating of conditions that focus on openness, variety, and supportability adds to the dynamic quality and life span of shared spaces. Whether it's a local area garden, a virtual care group, or a social celebration, the purposeful forming of these conditions cultivates a feeling of pride and divided liability between members.

As we ponder these tales, we perceive that the significance of a typical climate reaches out a long ways past the actual designs or virtual stages. Shared spaces act as pots where the human experience is molded, associations are framed, and the aggregate excursion of harmony unfurls. In the embroidery of life, these common spaces are the strings that mesh people into networks, networks into social orders, and social orders into a common mankind.

The investigation of tales that enlighten the significance of a typical climate, we should dive into stories that grandstand the effect of shared spaces on individual prosperity, cultural versatility, and the development of a common story.

Think about the narrative of a recreational area in a thickly populated metropolitan setting. Amidst substantial designs and occupied roads, the recreation area arises as a desert garden — a common space where people look for shelter from the rushing about of day to day existence. The plant life, seats, and strolling ways become a safe-haven for snapshots of isolation, exercise, and aggregate entertainment. In this metropolitan asylum, individuals from different backgrounds settle on something worth agreeing on, rising above financial contrasts in their common appreciation for nature and open spaces.

The recreation area isn't just an actual climate; it turns into a psychological and close to home shelter for those looking for reprieve. An individual, troubled by the burdens of work and individual difficulties, finds comfort underneath the shade of a tree. The demonstration of sitting on a recreation area seat, encompassed by the murmur of city life and the stirring of leaves, turns into a groundbreaking encounter. The common space of the recreation area, through its ability to offer serenity, outlines how normal conditions can add to mental prosperity and act as fundamental safe-havens for metropolitan occupants.

Conversely, the shortfall of shared spaces can uncover the void they leave in the texture of local area life. Picture a local where public social occasion spots have dwindled because of disregard or metropolitan turn of events. Occupants, once acquainted with unconstrained connections in collective spaces, wind up segregated inside the bounds of their homes. The story unfurls as people mourn the departure of a once-lively local area soul, stressing how the vanishing of shared spaces can disintegrate the social paste that ties neighbors together.

Additionally, the effect of shared spaces on cultural flexibility comes to the front in stories of catastrophe stricken networks. In the result of a cataclysmic event, for example, a storm or tremor, shared spaces become urgent center points for aggregate recuperation. A record unfurls in a public venue where dislodged occupants track down cover, share assets, and offer common help. The common climate turns into a help, offering actual security as well as close to home food in the midst of emergency.

Think about the flexibility of a beach front local area that climates the intermittent difficulties of typhoons. In this common climate, occupants meet up to strengthen their homes, share crisis supplies, and aggregately explore the vulnerabilities of outrageous climate occasions. The common experience of confronting misfortune cultivates a significant feeling of local area securities, featuring how normal conditions add to the versatility of people and networks despite outer difficulties.

The working environment, as a common climate, likewise assumes a crucial part in molding proficient elements and individual satisfaction. Tales from a cooperative office space highlight the groundbreaking force of shared workplaces. Here, representatives from different foundations and divisions wind up sharing thoughts, mastery, and a feeling of kinship. The open plan of the workplace cultivates unconstrained cooperations, prompting the cross-fertilization of thoughts that probably won't have happened in confined work areas.

Besides, the tale of a mentorship program inside this common work environment climate represents the potential for individual and expert development. An old pro and a newbie, united by the common space of the workplace, leave on a tutor mentee venture. The mentorship rises above customary progressive designs, establishing a climate where information streams naturally, and vocation improvement turns into an aggregate undertaking.

The common work environment climate turns into an impetus for mentorship, expertise sharing, and the development of a cooperative ethos.

In any case, the shift towards remote work, advanced quickly by worldwide occasions, acquaints new elements with the story of shared work areas. The story unfurls in a virtual gathering, where colleagues, topographically scattered, accumulate in a common computerized space. Notwithstanding actual distances, the common virtual climate turns into a course for cooperation, thought trade, and the upkeep of group union. The significance of a typical climate is re-imagined in the computerized scene, underlining the versatility of shared spaces to developing work patterns.

The story of a public kitchen inside a private complex adds a home-grown aspect to the investigation of shared conditions. In this common space, occupants, each with their culinary inclinations and social foundations, merge to get ready and offer dinners. The smell of different foods drifts through the air as neighbors trade recipes, cooking tips, and stories. The public kitchen turns into a microcosm of social trade, outlining how shared conditions inside private settings can cultivate a feeling of local area and diverse comprehension.

With regards to schooling, shared spaces reach out past homerooms to incorporate libraries, concentrate on regions, and common social event spots. The story unfurls in a college library, where understudies, fascinated in their examinations, establish a common climate that rises above disciplinary limits. The library turns into a center for interdisci-plinary cooperations, cooperative examination, and the cross-preparation of thoughts. In this common scholarly space, the quest for information turns into an aggregate undertaking, displaying the harmonious connec-tion between shared conditions and scholarly development.

Essentially, the story of an understudy drove drive to make a common report space features the organization of people in forming their common surroundings. Because of an absence of favorable review spaces nearby, understudies meet up to reuse an underutilized region into a dynamic report center. The common space turns into a demonstration of the groundbreaking effect of aggregate activity, showing how people, driven by a common objective, can shape their surroundings to address public issues.

Past the actual domain, virtual shared spaces in the domain of online training become instrumental in associating students across the globe. The story unfurls in a web-based course where members from assorted social foundations team up, talk about, and learn together. The common virtual climate turns into a stage for the trading of points of view, enhancing the instructive experience by integrating a worldwide aspect. In this unique circumstance, shared spaces rise above topographical con-straints, delineating the democratizing capability of advanced conditions in training.

Social establishments, like historical centers and exhibitions, give ex-traordinary shared spaces that work with social improvement and cultural reflection. Envision the story of a local area workmanship project facilitated by a neighborhood historical center. Inhabitants, paying little mind to imaginative foundation, meet up to add to an aggregate craftsmanship that mirrors the variety and solidarity of their local area. The common creative space turns into a material for individual articulation and a mirror mirroring the aggregate personality of the area.

In investigating the effect of shared conditions on social articulation, consider the tale of a road celebration celebrating social variety. Occupants, enhanced in customary clothing, share their music, dance, and culinary practices in an aggregate festival of social legacy. The common celebration space turns into an embroidery woven with strings of different societies, cultivating a deep satisfaction, understanding, and interconnectedness among local area individuals.

The meaning of shared spaces in forming social accounts is additionally exemplified in the narrative of a local area narrating project. In this drive, people of any age meet up to share individual accounts, tales, and oral chronicles. The common narrating climate turns into a storehouse of aggregate memory, safeguarding the extravagance of individual and local area encounters. It builds up the thought that common spaces, whether physical or computerized, assume a vital part in forming the social stories that characterize social orders.

In analyzing the accounts of shared spaces, it becomes apparent that these conditions are not aloof settings but rather unique cauldrons where individual stories meet, aggregate accounts unfurl, and cultural bonds are produced. Whether in the working environment, schooling, public kitchens, or social foundations, shared spaces act as the materials whereupon the human experience is painted with shared desires, cooperative undertakings, and the co-formation of significance.

As we explore the intricacies of the contemporary world, these stories highlight the persevering through significance of purposeful plan, inclusivity, and local area commitment inside shared spaces. The tales weave a story that stresses the requirement for shared conditions that rise above physical, social, and computerized limits. In doing as such, they enlighten the extraordinary capability of shared spaces to support prosperity, encourage strength, and add to the rich embroidered artwork of human association. As people proceed to shape and adjust shared spaces to address developing issues, the aggregate story of harmony unfurls, advising us that our common surroundings are the two reflections and modelers of the common human experience.

Chapter 2

"Traditions that Bind"

"Customs that Tight spot"

In the woven artwork of human life, customs arise as strings that wind around together the texture of societies, families, and networks. These persevering through customs, went down through ages, hold the ability to tie people, cultivate a feeling of having a place, and give an immortal association with the past. The investigation of customs discloses a rich embroidery of ceremonies, festivities, and practices that shape ways of life as well as act as scaffolds interfacing different social orders across reality.

Customs, established in history and culture, become vessels for the transmission of values and convictions. The story unfurls in a family kitchen, where a grandma gives the craft of setting up a mark dish to her grandkids. This culinary custom, went down through the ages, goes past the simple exchange of a recipe. It turns into an unmistakable connection to familial legacy, conveying with it the flavors, fragrances, and accounts of the people who preceded. The demonstration of getting ready and sharing this dish turns into a living practice that ties relatives together, making a common story woven with the strings of culinary inheritance.

In a more extensive cultural setting, the festival of strict celebrations turns into a sign of customs that tight spot networks. Think about the lively shades of a Diwali festivity, where families meet up to enlighten their homes with lights, trade desserts, and participate in customs that represent the victory of light over murkiness. The yearly recognition of strict customs turns into a common articulation of confidence, a common excursion that rises above individual convictions and interfaces followers in an aggregate festival of social character.

Customs stretch out their hug to critical life achievements, denoting the progression of time with ceremonies that tight spot people to their networks. The story unfurls in a wedding function, where revered traditions join two people in marriage. The trading of commitments, the wearing of formal clothing, and the emblematic ceremonies become strings woven into the texture of a common life. The wedding custom ties the couple as well as associates them to the more extensive local area, as loved ones accumulate to observe and participate in the euphoric association.

Language, as a living practice, turns into a strong power that ties networks and jam social personality. The story happens in a multigenerational family where a grandma imparts stories to her grandkids in a local tongue. This semantic custom turns into an extension across ages, guaranteeing the congruity of social legacy. The subtleties of language convey inside them the rhythm of familial stories, conventional stories, and the aggregate insight of progenitors, encouraging a significant association with social roots.

In the domain of schooling, scholarly customs act as soul changing experiences that tight spot understudies to a common excursion of learning. The story unfurls in a college beginning service, where graduates wear graduation outfits, get certificates, and throw their covers in the air in festival. This respected practice denotes the climax of scholastic pursuits, restricting understudies together in the common accomplishment of information and the expectation of future undertakings. The beginning function turns into an aggregate accentuation mark in the scholarly story, interfacing graduates across ages.

The work environment, as a microcosm of cultural cooperations, fosters own arrangement of customs tie partners and groups. Consider the casual practice of commending birthday events with shared cakes and warm words in the workplace lounge. This apparently basic demonstration turns into a custom that cultivates fellowship, fabricates relational associations, and adds to a positive work culture. The common experience of praising achievements frames a custom that rises above the expert domain, making bonds among partners that stretch out past the limits of the working environment.

Customary fine arts, gave over through ages, become articulations of social character and coherence. In a story set in a little town, craftsmans practice customary specialties that have been gone down through their families for a really long time.

The demonstration of making handwoven materials, earthenware, or multifaceted wood carvings turns into a living practice that ties the craftsmans to their social legacy. These artworks encapsulate not just the ability and creativity of the people yet additionally the aggregate insight and stylish inclinations of their precursors.

In investigating the meaning of customs that tight spot, recognizing the transaction among congruity and adaptation is fundamental. Customs, while established previously, are not static elements but rather living articulations that develop with the elements of society. The story unfurls locally that embraces the transformation of conventional practices to contemporary settings. A yearly gather celebration, for instance, may integrate present day components while holding the center ceremonies that praise overflow and appreciation. This powerful transaction among custom and development guarantees that social practices stay applicable and comprehensive across evolving times.

The story stretches out to intercultural customs that tight spot different networks through shared encounters. Consider a multicultural neighborhood where inhabitants meet up to sort out a yearly social trade fair. This custom permits people from various foundations to feature their traditions, cooking styles, and creative articulations. The fair turns into a common space where different practices cross, encouraging shared figuring out, regard, and a feeling of solidarity among local area individuals.

Besides, the practice of narrating turns into a general string that ties mankind across societies and ages. The story unfurls in a shared assembling where elderly folks pass down oral narratives to the more youthful age. Whether through fantasies, legends, or individual accounts, narrating customs act as stores of social information, moral lessons, and the aggregate memory of social orders. The demonstration of narrating rises above geological and transient limits, interfacing people to the more extensive human experience.

In investigating customs that dilemma, perceiving their job in molding a feeling of character and belonging is basic. The story happens in a diasporic local area where people, isolated from their genealogical countries, keep up with social customs for of safeguarding their character. Celebrations, customs, and language become life savers that associate diasporic networks to their underlying foundations, giving a feeling of coherence and having a place in new and new conditions.

The protection of native customs turns into a strong story that highlights the flexibility of networks notwithstanding outer tensions. In a story set in a native town, elderly folks give conventional natural information to more youthful ages. The occasional customs, land stewardship practices, and profound functions become customs that tight spot the local area not exclusively to their social legacy yet in addition to the land they possess. The cooperative connection between native customs and the common habitat mirrors a comprehensive comprehension of the interconnectedness, everything being equal.

Nonetheless, the account additionally investigates the fragile harmony between safeguarding customs and embracing cultural advancement. In a story set in a quickly urbanizing society, a local area wrestles with the test of saving customary practices despite modernization. The elderly folks, established in the insight of their predecessors, look for ways of coordinating conventional qualities into contemporary ways of life. This intergenerational exchange turns into a unique course of discussion, representing that practices, to stay pertinent, should adjust to changing cultural scenes while safeguarding their embodiment.

With regards to familial customs, the story unfurls in a family where the act of day to day family feasts turns into a valued practice. The demonstration of meeting up to share dinners, examine the occasions of the day, and reconnect as a family turns into a custom that ties ages. This custom not just supports actual prosperity through shared sustenance yet additionally develops close to home bonds and a feeling of familial solidarity. The supper table turns into a consecrated space where stories are traded, values are granted, and the progression of family customs is supported.

The investigation of customs that tight spot additionally stretches out to the domain of local area festivities. In a story set during a social celebration, the whole local area merges to take part in conventional moves, music, and collective dining experiences. The celebration turns into a common encounter that encourages a feeling of aggregate euphoria, building up friendly bonds and a common social character. The cadenced pulsates of customary music reverberation the heartbeat of the local area, representing the essentialness and coherence of social practices.

The practice of collective chipping in fills in as a story that delineates the limiting power of shared values and unselfishness. Locally where people meet up to take part in aggregate demonstrations of administration, whether through natural drives, good cause work, or supporting nearby causes, a custom of shared liability arises. The demonstration of rewarding the local area turns into a common worth that ties people in a typical reason, encouraging a feeling of social union and obligation.

Besides, the investigation of strict journey customs uncovers how shared profound excursions can tie people and networks. In a story set during a yearly journey, individuals from different foundations embrace a sacrosanct excursion to a worshipped site. The journey turns into a common articulation of confidence, solidarity, and shared commitment. Explorers, regardless of their fluctuated educational encounters, find a shared trait in the otherworldly journey that tough situations them together on a holy journey course.

The custom of mentorship arises as a story that delineates the intergenerational bonds fashioned through shared information and direction. In an expert setting, old pros assume the job of coaches, passing down their skill, experiences, and profession exhortation to more youthful partners. This custom of mentorship adds to proficient improvement as well as makes a feeling of progression and interconnectedness inside the expert local area.

The investigation of sports customs uncovers how shared excitement for athletic undertakings can tie networks and countries. In a story set during a significant game, fans from different foundations meet up to help their groups. The custom of sports being a fan turns into a binding together power that rises above social, etymological, and international contrasts, making a common space where people can communicate their aggregate pride and enthusiasm.

Customs that tight spot likewise track down articulation in the domain of natural stewardship. In a story set locally dedicated to economical practices, a custom of environmental obligation arises. The common endeavors to safeguard regular assets, diminish natural effect, and participate in economical practices become strings that tight spot people in a typical obligation to the prosperity of the planet. This custom of ecological stewardship mirrors a common worth framework that rises above individual interests for a long term benefit.

Investigation of "Customs that Tight spot," we dig into the accounts of versatility, change, and the transaction between individual organization and common bonds inside the setting of customs.

In a story set in a little town going through monetary changes, the practice of collective cultivating becomes the dominant focal point. As the local area faces difficulties presented by current agrarian practices and monetary movements, residents meet up to maintain the well established practice of mutual cultivating. The practice turns into an image of versatility, epitomizing the aggregate soul of the local area to adjust to outside pressures while saving their agrarian legacy. The demonstration of planting, collecting, and sharing the yield turns into a custom that ties the local area in a common obligation to support their lifestyle.

Inside familial practices, a story unfurls in a family where individuals, scattered across various urban communities and nations, rejoin yearly for a loved custom — family narrating night. Notwithstanding the actual distances, the custom of narrating turns into a binding together power that interfaces ages. Through tales, recollections, and shared giggling, relatives span the holes made by reality. The narrating custom turns into a demonstration of the persevering through force of familial bonds and the purposeful endeavors to safeguard shared stories.

In the domain of native practices, the story is set against a scenery of social rejuvenation. A people group, confronting the disintegration of its conventional practices because of outside impacts, leaves on an excursion to recover and resuscitate their genealogical traditions. Seniors pass on conventional biological information, hallowed services are reestablished, and the more youthful age effectively partakes during the time spent social rebuilding. This story highlights the organization of networks in safeguarding and restoring their customs as a wellspring of solidarity and flexibility.

The custom of craftsmanship arises as a topic in a story set in a quickly industrializing society. Craftsmans, whose conventional artworks are in danger of oldness, enhance to adjust their abilities to contemporary requests. The custom of craftsmanship turns into a unique power, showing the way that customs can develop without losing their pith. The craftsmans explore the fragile harmony between safeguarding the realness of their art and embracing development, displaying the strength of customs notwithstanding cultural changes.

Inside the setting of strict customs, the story unfurls locally that wrestles with changing socioeconomics and developing profound practices. Because of these movements, the practice of interfaith discourse flourishes, encouraging common comprehension and cooperation among assorted strict networks. The exchange turns into a common space where people, in spite of their contrasting convictions, find shared belief and foster an aggregate obligation to harmony and conjunction. The practice of interfaith discourse turns into a scaffold that ties people across strict partitions.

The working environment, as a microcosm of cultural elements, witnesses a story where an organization custom of mentorship is instrumental in exploring hierarchical changes. In the midst of rebuilding and changes, prepared representatives coach their more youthful partners, giving direction and backing. The mentorship custom turns into a course for information move and hierarchical congruity, showing how work environment customs add to the strength and flexibility of an expert local area.

With regards to municipal commitment, a local area custom of official Q&A events turns into a story point of convergence. As cultural issues emerge, occupants meet up to participate in open conversations, share viewpoints, and on the whole location challenges. The practice of municipal events turns into a sign of majority rule values, underlining the significance of mutual cooperation in dynamic cycles. The common space of the municipal center turns into an image of city solidarity and cooperative critical thinking.

In the computerized age, the story unfurls in a web-based local area where the custom of virtual book clubs flourishes. Perusers from various corners of the world interface through computerized stages to examine writing, trade thoughts, and cultivate a feeling of scholarly kinship. The virtual book club custom turns into an outline of how innovation can be bridled to make shared spaces that rise above geological constraints, permitting people to bond over a common love for writing.

The practice of social trade becomes the overwhelming focus in a story where networks from different foundations meet up to coordinate a yearly multicultural celebration. Through music, dance, food, and workmanship, members commend the wealth of their particular societies while fashioning associations across social limits. The multicultural celebration custom turns into a dynamic articulation of solidarity in variety, exhibiting how shared social encounters add to cultural union.

Inside the setting of natural stewardship, a story unfurls locally that embraces the practice of tree-establishing services. Inhabitants, youthful and old, meet up to establish saplings, making a practice that represents their obligation to ecological maintainability. The demonstration of planting turns into a custom that ties people to the common obligation of safeguarding the regular world, representing how ecological practices can move aggregate activity for everyone's best interests.

The practice of local area driven drives turns into a focal subject in a story set in a metropolitan area confronting improvement. Not entirely settled to protect the personality of their local area, start activities, for example, local area gardens, craftsmanship establishments, and neighborhood tidy up endeavors. These grassroots practices become a type of aggregate obstruction, exhibiting the force of networks to shape their own stories and safeguard the quintessence of their common spaces.

In investigating the extraordinary capability of customs, the story movements to a local area that reclassifies its practice of special festivals. Rather than conventional gift trades, the local area chooses to zero in on thoughtful gestures and beneficent commitments during the happy season. This extraordinary practice mirrors a cognizant decision to move the accentuation from realism to upsides of sympathy and local area administration, featuring how customs can be purposefully adjusted to line up with developing cultural qualities.

The practice of narrating takes a computerized turn in a story set in a web-based local area where people share individual stories through online journals, web recordings, and virtual entertainment. The computerized narrating custom turns into a stage for self-articulation, association, and the production of a virtual common space where different stories merge. This contemporary variation of narrating customs highlights the ease of customs in adjusting to the advancing methods of correspondence and articulation.

The story of a social renaissance unfurls locally that rediscovers and resuscitates failed to remember imaginative practices. Through cooperative endeavors, people revive customary works of art, guaranteeing their congruity for people in the future. This story represents how customs, when effectively embraced and revived, become impetuses for social restoration, adding to the social energy of a local area.

In a story set in a globalized world, the custom of language safeguarding turns into an account center. As dialects face the gamble of annihilation, networks effectively work to report, instruct, and rejuvenate their local tongues. The custom of language conservation turns into a vital part of social personality, associating people to their phonetic legacy and cultivating a deep satisfaction in etymological variety.

The investigation of extraordinary customs likewise dives into the story of a local area that reconsiders its way to deal with compromise. Rather than propagating verifiable hostilities, the local area embraces the practice of peacebuilding circles, giving a space to open exchange and compromise. This extraordinary custom turns into a demonstration of the force of deliberate endeavors to break the pattern of contention and fabricate extensions of understanding.

In a story set in a quickly changing mechanical scene, the custom of expertise sharing arises as a reaction to the difficulties of robotization and occupation dislodging. People meet up to share their abilities, information, and mastery, making a practice of cooperative learning and versatility. This story highlights the job of customs in encouraging versatility and aggregate reactions to cultural movements.

The custom of local area care turns into a focal topic in a story where neighbors effectively support each other during seasons of individual or aggregate difficulties. This custom of common guide and fortitude represents the significance of building shared networks that stretch out past individual interests. The common obligation to local area care turns into a limiting power that builds up friendly bonds and flexibility.

he investigation of "Customs that Tight spot" envelops a different cluster of stories that highlight the strength, flexibility, and extraordinary capability of customs across different circles of human existence. From familial narrating to ecological stewardship, from working environment mentorship to social rejuvenation, customs assume a diverse part in forming personalities, cultivating associations, and adding to the common stories of networks. As people and social orders explore the intricacies of the contemporary world, the customs that tight spot stay strings of coherence as well as instruments of positive change, showing the persevering through limit of shared practices to enhance the human experience.

2.1 Examination of family traditions and rituals.

"Assessment of Family Customs and Ceremonies"

In the cozy spaces of home, family customs and ceremonies arise as ageless strings that weave the texture of shared encounters, values, and associations. These traditions, went down through ages, shape the character of families and give a feeling of coherence in the midst of the rhythmic movement of life. This investigation dives into the rich embroidery of family customs and ceremonies, disentangling stories that enlighten their importance in encouraging familial bonds, sending values, and making a feeling of having a place.

The story starts in a family kitchen, where the matron gives the custom of a Sunday family dinner. Across ages, relatives accumulate to share a good dinner, trading stories, giggling, and warmth. The clunking of utensils and the fragrance of recognizable dishes become tactile markers of this valued practice, restricting relatives in a common encounter of sustenance and association.

The Sunday family feast fills in as a ritualized assembling, rising above the everyday practice of day to day existence to make a space for shared minutes and a feeling of familial fellowship.

Inside the setting of familial festivals, the story unfurls in the arrangements for a yearly family get-together. This custom, set apart by giggling, games, and the sharing of family stories, turns into a standard for connection. The family gathering serves as a bubbly event as well as a custom of reaffirming the ties that tight spot family members together across time and distance. Through the trading of photos, recipes, and stories, relatives add to the living file of shared encounters, supporting a feeling of having a place that reaches out past individual lifetimes.

A more profound assessment of family customs brings us into the domain of social legacy and its part in forming familial personality. In a story set inside an outsider family, the practice of celebrating social celebrations turns into a critical connection to familial roots. The family explores the fragile harmony between digestion into another culture and the safeguarding of customs that associate them to their legacy. The social celebrations become events for passing down language, customs, and values, cultivating a deep satisfaction and congruity notwithstanding social development.

Likewise, the story unfurls in a family where the custom of narrating turns into a method for communicating familial history. The older folks accumulate the more youthful age, retelling stories of predecessors, familial victories, and difficulties survive. Through the oral custom of narrating, relatives acquire an ordered record of their heredity as well as the ethos, values, and versatility that characterize their familial personality. The narrating custom turns into a living vault of the family's aggregate memory, building up a common story that ties ages together.

In investigating the crossing point of family customs and individual achievements, the story takes us to the custom of birthday festivities. Past the cake and candles, birthday celebrations become an event for the family to meet up and communicate love, appreciation, and certification. The practice of commending birthday events fills in as a yearly custom of recognizing every relative's uniqueness and commitment to the familial embroidery. Through shared dinners, smart presents, and genuine wishes, birthday celebrations become snapshots of aggregate festival that reinforce familial bonds.

The assessment of family customs reaches out to the ceremonies related with significant life advances, like weddings. In a story revolved around wedding arrangements, the many-sided traditions, services, and ceremonies become strings that weave a story of association and progression. The trading of promises, the wearing of stylized clothing, and the support of relatives in customary rituals make a stately space that rises above individual associations to underscore the interconnectedness of families. The wedding custom turns into a critical marker in the continuum of familial life, representing the extension and development of the nuclear family.

Inside the space of despondency and misfortune, the account investigates the customs of grieving and recognition. Despite a family misfortune, the practice of meeting up for remembrance administrations and celebrations turns into a wellspring of comfort and backing. The ceremonies related with misfortune give an organized structure to communicating pain, sharing recollections, and looking for aggregate strength. The collective demonstration of recollecting turns into a ritualized interaction through which families explore the intricacies of misfortune while confirming the persevering through bonds that interface them.

An impactful investigation of familial customs unfurls with regards to special festivals. Whether established in strict observances, social celebrations, or common customs, occasions become markers of shared happiness, reflection, and association. The story navigates the arrangements for a bubbly season, catching the ceremonies of designing the home, planning extraordinary dinners, and participating in aggregate exercises. The practice of special festivals fills in as a social anchor, giving families a common schedule that intersperses the progression of time and encourages a feeling of congruity across ages.

The assessment of family customs reaches out to the homegrown ceremonies that pervade regular daily existence with importance and importance. In a story set inside a family, the morning schedule turns into a ceremonial space where relatives join before the day unfurls. The common demonstrations of breakfast planning, easygoing discussions, and the trading of morning good tidings become miniature customs that set the vibe for the afternoon and build up the familial texture. These everyday ceremonies, frequently underestimated, add to the unpretentious however significant manners by which families associate in the beat of day to day existence.

The investigation of family customs drives us to the idea of inheritance and the ceremonies related with passing down legacies, values, and intelligence. In a story set in a tribal home, the custom of giving over a loved family curio turns into an emblematic demonstration of entrusting the more youthful age with the obligation of saving familial history. The passing down of treasures, whether substantial or elusive, turns into a custom that rises above material belongings, typifying the congruity of familial character.

A more profound assessment of family customs digs into the elements of generational movements and the development of familial traditions. The story unfurls in a family where more youthful individuals challenge specific customs while trying to lay out their own. The intergenerational discourse turns into a unique interaction through which families arrange the pressure between saving the past and adjusting to the present. The development of family customs mirrors the strength of familial bonds in obliging assorted points of view and guaranteeing the pertinence of customs across evolving times.

The assessment of family customs reaches out to the ceremonies related with supper time. In a story based on the supper table, the demonstration of meeting up for dinners turns into a custom that rises above sustenance. The common dinners give a space to discussion, chuckling, and the trading of day to day encounters. The custom of family meals turns into a ritualized assembling that cultivates correspondence, solidarity, and a feeling of public prosperity.

The story investigates the custom of family get-aways for of holding and making enduring recollections. Whether it's a yearly ocean side excursion, a mountain retreat, or a social investigation, the family get-away turns into a ritualized escape from schedule. The common encounters, experiences, and difficulties looked during excursions add to the production of an aggregate story that supports familial bonds and makes a repository of shared recollections.

Inside the setting of instructive practices, the story unfurls in a family where the custom of cultivating an affection for learning turns into a focal concentration. The common exercises of perusing together, captivating in instructive games, and supporting each other's scholastic interests become customs that underline the worth of information and scholarly interest. The instructive customs inside the family add to a culture of deep rooted learning and the transmission of scholastic qualities across ages.

An investigation of family customs wouldn't be finished without looking at the ceremonies related with social variety and mixed families. In a story set in a multicultural family, the family takes part in customs that draw from various social foundations. The festival of different celebrations, the consideration of customary cooking styles, and the fuse of customs from different legacies become ceremonies that commend the lavishness of social variety inside the family. Mixed families explore the combination of customs, making a one of a kind embroidery that mirrors the mixture of different impacts.

The story goes to the idea of making new practices inside families, especially with regards to forward thinking family structures. In a story revolved around picked families and steady networks, people manufacture customs that go past customary standards. The festival of companionship commemorations, the foundation of collective ceremonies, and the deliberate development of picked familial securities become accounts that challenge customary meanings of family while underscoring the persevering through need for association and having a place.

The assessment of family customs stretches out to the computerized domain, where innovation turns into a channel for keeping up with familial associations. In a story set in a world interconnected through computerized stages, the custom of virtual family social events becomes the dominant focal point. Video calls, shared advanced collections, and online festivals become ceremonies that span geological distances, permitting families to remain associated in the virtual space. The mix of innovation into familial practices mirrors the versatility of customs to the developing methods of correspondence.

The account investigates the ceremonies related with soul changing experiences inside families, especially the progress from pre-adulthood to adulthood. In a story about growing up, the family custom of celebrating huge achievements like graduations, first positions, or individual accomplishments turns into a transitional experience that denotes the singular's entrance into another period of life. The customs related with these achievements act as representative markers of development and achievement inside the familial story.

A top to bottom assessment of family customs incorporates the ceremonies related with the safeguarding of social and familial accounts. In an account based on a family document, the custom of keeping up with photograph collections, set up accounts, and oral chronicles turns into a conscious demonstration of narrating. The documented customs act as a vault of familial accounts, guaranteeing that the tales of predecessors, significant occasions, and shared encounters are safeguarded for people in the future. The demonstration of returning to the family file turns into a custom of association with the past and an affirmation of the continuous story of the family.

Inside the setting of providing care, the story unfurls in a family where the custom of supporting older individuals turns into a focal concentration. The customs related with really focusing on maturing guardians or grandparents become demonstrations of affection, correspondence, and familial obligation. The providing care customs inside the family mirror the intergenerational bonds that support people through the various periods of life, building up the repetitive idea of familial help.

An assessment of family customs wouldn't be finished disregarding the ceremonies related with the discussion of social, strict, or philosophical contrasts inside families. In a story set in a family with different conviction frameworks, the family takes part in the custom of open exchange and shared regard. The customs of celebrating different strict celebrations, recognizing assorted points of view, and figuring out something worth agreeing on become ceremonies that encourage understanding and solidarity inside the familial setting.

The story digs into the idea of familial versatility and the job of customs in exploring difficulties. In a story set during a time of misfortune, the family custom of flexibility becomes clear in the ceremonies of supporting each other, tracking down strength in shared esteems, and adjusting to evolving conditions. The familial strength custom fills in as a story of perseverance, representing how families draw on their common history to beat snags and arise more grounded.

An investigation of family customs stretches out to the ceremonies related with the progression of time and the affirmation of generational inheritances. In a story based on generational changes, the family participates in customs that commend the achievements of the most youthful individuals while respecting the insight of the older folks.

The ceremonies related with birthday celebrations, commemorations, and family social events become snapshots of reflection, appreciation, and the transmission of familial favors across the ages.

The story goes to the idea of purposeful residing inside families, where the custom of care turns into a focal concentration. In a story set in a family rehearsing purposeful living, the customs of day to day reflections, shared objectives, and public care practices become customs that shape the family's aggregate story. The deliberate living custom highlights the family's obligation to encouraging significant associations, intentional activities, and a common vision for a satisfying life.

An assessment of family customs wouldn't be finished disregarding the ceremonies related with the cultivating of imagination and individual articulation. In a story based on imaginative pursuits, the family custom of empowering imagination becomes obvious in the ceremonies of craftsmanship evenings, shared exhibitions, and cooperative ventures. The creative practices inside the family add to a culture that values self-articulation, development, and the festival of individual gifts.

The story investigates the idea of versatile practices inside families, especially with regards to changing cultural standards. In a story set in a family exploring developing orientation jobs, the custom of testing generalizations and cultivating balance turns into a focal concentration. The ceremonies related with engaging every relative, regardless of orientation, become a purposeful work to reclassify familial customs in arrangement with moderate qualities.

Inside the setting of natural cognizance, the story unfurls in a family where the custom of reasonable residing turns into a point of convergence. The customs related with eco-accommodating practices, local area tidy up drives, and natural instruction become customs that mirror the family's obligation to mindful stewardship. The natural practices inside the family add to a story that adjusts familial qualities to a more extensive ethos of maintainability.

The investigation of family customs stretches out to the ceremonies related with innovation utilization and its effect on familial associations. In a story set in an educated family, the family custom of laying out without tech zones and assigned screen times turns into a purposeful work to cultivate up close and personal collaborations and careful commitment. The tech-cognizant practices inside the family mirror a familiarity with the likely impacts of innovation on familial connections and the deliberate development of equilibrium.

An assessment of family customs incorporates the ceremonies related with the idea of appreciation and the affirmation of shared gifts. In a story revolved around the practice of communicating much obliged, the family takes part in ceremonies of appreciation diaries, common articulations of appreciation, and thoughtful gestures.

The appreciation customs inside the family add to a story that stresses the benefit of recognizing and praising the wealth of shared encounters.

Inside the setting of present day versatility and worldwide associations, the account investigates the practice of remaining associated across geological distances. In a story set in a family scattered across various landmasses, the practice of normal virtual family get-togethers turns into a help for keeping up with familial bonds. The ceremonies of video calls, internet games, and shared computerized spaces become customs that rise above actual distances, permitting relatives to remain associated notwithstanding the difficulties of worldwide versatility.

An inside and out assessment of family customs reaches out to the ceremonies related with compromise and the cultivating of solid correspondence. In a story based on the custom of family gatherings, the ceremonies of open discourse, undivided attention, and cooperative critical thinking become deliberate endeavors to support familial congruity. The compromise customs inside the family add to a story that esteems the significance of tending to contrasts with deference and understanding.

The account goes to the idea of advancing family structures and the variation of customs to oblige assorted meanings of connection. In a story set in a modern family, the practice of inclusivity becomes obvious in the customs of celebrating picked relatives, perceiving different familial bonds, and purposefully making a space that embraces different types of associations. The comprehensive customs inside the family mirror a deliberate work to reclassify familial stories in arrangement with contemporary understandings of family.

2.2 Stories of how these traditions strengthen familial bonds.

"Accounts of How Customs Fortify Familial Bonds"

In the core of familial stories, customs arise as strong impetuses, winding around strings of association and strength that persevere through time. These accounts dive into the mind boggling embroidery of familial customs, investigating how these respected practices become more than ceremonies — they become stories that reinforce the obligations of connection, encourage flexibility, and make a common feeling of personality.

The excursion starts in an unassuming kitchen where the matron, Maria, carefully follows a recipe went down through ages. Sunday mornings in the Ramirez family are inseparable from the custom of creating natively constructed tamales. The musical hints of giggling and the sweet-smelling orchestra of flavors swirl around as numerous ages accumulate to participate in this culinary custom. Maria, with hands endured by long stretches of custom, confers the culinary mysteries as well as the narratives of progenitors who tracked down comfort and happiness in the specialty of cooking. As hands meet up to overlay corn husks, the demonstration turns out to be more than culinary mastery — it turns into a common dance of shared legacy, love, and the continuation of a custom that has invigorated familial ties for ages.

Inside the practice of the yearly family get-together, the Parker family winds around a story of association that traverses ages. As the sun plunges underneath the skyline, projecting a warm shine on the assembled family members, the Parkers take part in a custom of narrating. Every relative contributes a section to the aggregate story, recapping stories of wins, difficulties, and minutes that characterize their common history. The custom of narrating during the family get-together changes the occasion from a simple social event into a living annal of the family's excursion. More youthful individuals find motivation in the adventures of versatility described by their older folks, understanding that the strength of familial securities lies in the present as well as in the reverberations of stories that resound through time.

In a settler family, the Patel family maintains the practice of Diwali, the Celebration of Lights. As the smell of flavors blends with the lively tints of rangoli, three ages accumulate to praise the victory of light over murkiness. The practice of Diwali isn't simply a social praise; a demonstration of the familial strength rises above geological limits. For the Patels, Diwali turns into a holy second where familial bonds are enlightened, manufacturing an association between the underlying foundations of their legacy and the parts of their diasporic venture. The glimmering diyas light up the room as well as enlighten the common account of the Patel family's perseverance and solidarity.

In the peaceful setting of the Anderson family home, the custom of sleep time narrating unfurls. Every evening, as the kids settle under comfortable covers, their grandma, a caretaker of family legend, winds around charming stories. These are not simple stories; they are customs given over through ages. The characters in these stories are not fictitious; they are precursors, each with an illustration to grant. Through the practice of sleep time narrating, the Anderson family supports a feeling of having a place that rises above time. The youthful ones, spellbound by stories of boldness and love, retain the accounts as well as the implicit commitment that familial bonds persevere through the ages.

In the midst of the wonder of a family wedding, the Johnsons take part in the custom of the solidarity flame function. As the lady of the hour and husband to be each take a lit light and together fuel a third, a fire that represents their association, the demonstration turns out to be more significant than a marital custom. It turns into a visual similitude for the combination of two families into one. The glimmering fire addresses the common eventual fate of the couple as well as the interlacing predeterminations of the Johnson and Smith families. The solidarity candle service rises above the big day, making a permanent imprint on the aggregate story of familial solidarity and shared desires.

In the calm minutes before sleep time, the Turner family accumulates for a daily custom of appreciation. Every relative alternates communicating what they are appreciative for that day. This basic practice, brought into the world from the craving to cultivate appreciation, changes the unremarkable into the sacrosanct. The demonstration of recognizing and sharing appreciation turns into an everyday indication of the favors woven into the texture of their lives.

The Turner family ritualizes appreciation, developing an aggregate story that focuses on appreciation, versatility, and the acknowledgment that familial bonds are reinforced through a common affirmation of life's overflow.

Inside the Thompson family, the custom of a yearly setting up camp excursion unfurls as an adventure of experience and harmony. For three ages, the Thompsons have withdrawn to a similar spot, settled by a quiet lake. The snapping of the open air fire turns into a chorale to stories shared under a twilight sky. The practice of setting up camp fills in as a conscious decision to get away from the commotion of current life and submerge themselves in nature. It turns into a journey, to an actual area, yet to a space where familial bonds are produced through shared chuckling, marshmallow-simmering meetings, and the aggregate wonderment motivated by the loftiness of the normal world.

In a family where scholarly greatness is venerated, the custom of a family concentrate on night turns into a story of aggregate quest for information. The Barnes family, mindful of the extraordinary force of training, saves one night seven days devoted to shared concentrate on meetings. The calm murmur of turning pages and a periodic trade of experiences make an environment where the quest for information isn't single however shared. The custom of family concentrate on night builds up the ethos that scholarly development is a common undertaking, cultivating a story that values instruction as a limiting power that rises above individual accomplishments.

For the Garcia family, the custom of a yearly beneficent task has turned into a story of sympathy and benevolence. Whether it's chipping in at a neighborhood cover, sorting out a local area cleanup, or taking part in a foundation run, the Garcias purposefully commit time to offer in return. The demonstration of serving others turns into a custom that fortifies familial securities as well as imparts a common feeling of obligation toward the more extensive local area. Through these magnanimous customs, the Garcia family winds around a story that underlines the significance of sympathy, liberality, and the comprehension that familial bonds reach out past direct relations.

The custom of a week after week family game night unfurls in the Smith family as an energetic story of well disposed contest and shared euphoria. Every week, the family assembles around a table loaded down with prepackaged games, cards, and giggling. The practice of game night isn't just about winning or losing; it's tied in with making a space where familial bonds are built up through energy and shared snapshots of cheerfulness. The Smith family's obligation to game night turns into a demonstration of the conviction that delight, in its least complex structure, is a strong paste that ties families together.

In a family where imaginative articulation is commended, the practice of a family craftsmanship day turns into a story of innovativeness, investigation, and shared self-articulation.

The Robinsons put away a day every month to participate in different creative undertakings — painting, chiseling, or even cooperative ventures. The practice of family craftsmanship day isn't restricted to the dominance of imaginative abilities; it is tied in with making a space where every relative's extraordinary voice is energized and celebrated. Through this custom, the Robinson family supports a story that values independence and the common quest for inventive articulation.

Inside the Kent family, the custom of a yearly family retreat unfurls as a story of reflection and deliberate association. As the relatives accumulate in a tranquil retreat place, the center movements from the interruptions of day to day existence to shared snapshots of thought. The custom of the family retreat turns into a purposeful decision to turn off, reflect, and participate in open discussions. The retreat fills in as a reset button, permitting every relative to add to an aggregate story of development, understanding, and the reaffirmation of familial bonds.

Notwithstanding misfortune, the custom of a week after week family flexibility circle turns into a story of help, strength, and shared backbone. The Thompsons, exploring a difficult period, assemble every week to share their battles, wins, and desires. The custom of the flexibility circle isn't tied in with limiting difficulties however turning around them together. The common space turns into a safe-haven where weakness is met with understanding, and familial bonds are sustained through shared help. The Thompson family's obligation to flexibility turns into a story that highlights that strength is definitely not a singular property however an aggregate undertaking.

The practice of family film night unfurls in the Pastry specialist family as a story of shared diversion, giggling, and holding. As the lights faint and the screen glimmers to life, the Cooks leave on a realistic excursion that rises above simple diversion. The practice of film night turns into an organized investigation of shared stories, chuckling, and the making of an aggregate story that reaches out past the bounds of the screen. Through this practice, the Dough punchers develop a space where familial bonds are reinforced through the wizardry of narrating.

Inside the Hamilton family, the practice of a month to month family meeting turns into a story of open correspondence, independent direction, and the encouraging of shared liability. As relatives assemble around a table, the environment is one of coordinated effort as opposed to ordered progression. The practice of the family meeting guarantees that everybody's voice is heard, making a space where familial choices are made on the whole. The Hamiltons' obligation to open correspondence turns into a story that underscores the significance of shared liability, straightforwardness, and the comprehension that familial bonds flourish in a climate of common regard.

In a family that values wellbeing and health, the custom of a week by week family wellness meeting turns into a story of aggregate prosperity and shared obligation to wellbeing.

Whether it's a family climb, a gathering exercise, or a yoga meeting in the parlor, the Johnsons deliberately put away opportunity for actual work. The practice of family wellness isn't just about the quest for individual wellbeing; it's tied in with making a space where familial bonds are reinforced through shared objectives, consolation, and the festival of prosperity as an aggregate accomplishment.

The practice of celebrating individual accomplishments unfurls in the Ross family as a story of shared pride, consolation, and familial help. As every relative achieves an individual objective, whether it's acing a test, finishing a task, or accomplishing a wellness achievement, the Ross family accumulates to celebrate. The practice of recognizing individual accomplishments turns into a purposeful work to cultivate a culture where familial bonds are strengthened through shared acknowledgment and support. Through this practice, the Ross family develops a story that esteems every part's one of a kind excursion and the aggregate satisfaction got from individual victories.

In the tranquil snapshots of the night, the custom of a sleep time cradlesong turns into a story of solace, love, and the greatness of ages. As the matron of the Green family supports her grandkid, she delicately sings a bedtime song went down through the family. The custom of the sleep time children's song isn't just about mitigating to rest; it's tied in with making a space where familial bonds are woven through the delicate tunes that have reverberated as the years progressed. The Green family's obligation to the sleep time bedtime song turns into a story that traverses ages, a living demonstration of the persevering through force of shared love and solace.

The practice of a yearly family vision board unfurls in the Williams family as a story of shared dreams, desires, and deliberate objective setting. As relatives accumulate with magazines, scissors, and paste, the environment is accused of a feeling of direction. The practice of the family vision board isn't bound to living in fantasy land; it's tied in with making a space where familial bonds are fortified through shared dreams representing things to come. Through this practice, the Williams family develops a story that values purposefulness, aggregate dreaming, and the comprehension that familial bonds are improved through a common obligation to development.

In a family where natural cognizance is a core value, the custom of a month to month family eco-challenge turns into a story of shared liability and supportability. The Mill operator family, mindful of the effect of individual activities in the world, takes part in a month to month challenge to decrease their ecological impression. The custom of the family eco-challenge isn't just about biological care; it's tied in with making a space where familial bonds are reinforced through shared responsibilities to maintainable residing. Through this custom, the Mill operator family winds around a story that values ecological stewardship as an aggregate liability.

Inside the Davis family, the practice of a yearly family legacy day unfurls as a story of social festival, schooling, and the transmission of familial information. As relatives assemble to investigate their social roots through food, music, and stories, the environment is energetic with a feeling of association. The practice of family legacy day isn't bound to the past; it's tied in with making a space where familial bonds are enhanced through the festival of social variety. Through this custom, the Davis family develops a story that esteems the significance of knowing one's foundations and the common pride that comes from respecting hereditary practices.

The practice of a month to month family volunteer day unfurls in the Thompson family as a story of shared sympathy, local area commitment, and the development of a feeling of obligation. As the relatives commit a day every month to charitable effort, the climate is accused of a feeling of giving. The practice of family volunteer day isn't just about selflessness; it's tied in with making a space where familial bonds are fortified through shared thoughtful gestures. Through this custom, the Thompson family winds around a story that values social obligation as an aggregate undertaking.

In the quiet snapshots of the time of rest, the custom of a week after week family petitioning heaven time turns into a story of otherworldly association, reflection, and the cultivating of shared confidence. As the Johnson family assembles briefly of petition, the air is permeated with a feeling of respect. The custom of family petitioning God time isn't restricted to strict ceremonies; it's tied in with making a space where familial bonds are woven through shared snapshots of otherworldly association. Through this custom, the Johnson family develops a story that esteems the significance of shared confidence and the comprehension that familial bonds are strengthened through otherworldly solidarity.

The custom of a yearly family time case unfurls in the Carter family as a story of reflection, expectation, and the conservation of recollections. As relatives contribute things, notes, and keepsakes to the time case, the climate is loaded up with a feeling of custom. The custom of the family time case isn't restricted to sentimentality; it's tied in with making a space where familial bonds are enhanced through the purposeful conservation of minutes. Through this custom, the Carter family winds around a story that esteems the repeating idea of time and the common affirmation that familial bonds rise above fleeting limits.

In a family that loves human expression, the practice of a yearly family ability show turns into a story of imagination, support, and the festival of individual gifts. As relatives exhibit their gifts, whether it's singing, moving, or performing wizardry deceives, the climate is buzzing with a feeling of brotherhood. The custom of the family ability show isn't bound to diversion; it's tied in with making a space where familial bonds are fortified through the festival of every part's one of a kind capacities. Through this custom, the Johnson family develops a story that esteems the significance of self-articulation and the comprehension that familial bonds are enhanced through the affirmation of individual gifts.

2.3 Reflections on the role of shared rituals in creating joy.

"Reflections on the Job of Shared Customs in Making Delight"

In the woven artwork of human experience, shared ceremonies arise as strings that mesh happiness into the texture of our lives. These customs, whether went down through ages or made again, act as channels for shared snapshots of association, festivity, and importance. This investigation considers the significant job of shared ceremonies in cultivating delight inside the multifaceted elements of human connections and mutual encounters.

At the core of this reflection is the custom of a Sunday family early lunch — a private practice where ages accumulate around a loaded table to eat and share giggling. The clunking of utensils, the smell of newly prepared espresso, and the ensemble of voices mixing in amicable discussion make a sacrosanct space of harmony. The Sunday informal breakfast custom turns into a supply of satisfaction, a desert garden where familial bonds are supported, and the straightforward demonstration of sharing a feast changes into a festival of association.

The excursion of euphoria stretches out to the domain of social festivals, where the custom of a yearly celebration turns into a dynamic articulation of shared character and extravagance. Whether it's the cheerful shades of Holi, the cadenced beats of a customary dance, or the exquisite joys of bubbly foods, the social celebration custom turns into a tangible gala that rises above individual encounters. The common festival turns into a blissful confirmation of social legacy, joining networks in an aggregate articulation of pride and having a place.

Inside the familial story, the reflection goes to the practice of a week after week game evening. As relatives assemble around a board or game, the air is loaded up with cordial chitchat, key reasoning, and the common rush of contest. The game night custom turns into a wellspring of satisfaction that rises above age obstructions, encouraging intergenerational bonds and making enduring recollections. Through the happiness of play, the family custom turns into a demonstration of the getting through euphoria tracked down in shared snapshots of chuckling and cordial competition.

With regards to individual achievements, the reflection goes to the custom of a graduation service. The expectation, the wearing of graduation outfits, and the aggregate commendation become ceremonies that hoist the singular achievement to a common festival. The graduation service turns into an upbeat accentuation mark in the familial story, representing scholarly accomplishment as well as the aggregate help, pride, and shared dreams that float the alumni on their excursion.

The investigation of shared customs reaches out to the common domain, where the custom of a town fair turns into an aggregate festival of local area soul.

The fragrance of cotton treats, the vivid merry go round, and the chuckling of neighbors make a bubbly environment that rises above individual contrasts. The town fair custom turns into an euphoric embroidery of shared encounters, cultivating a feeling of solidarity and association that goes past the transient snapshots of the occasion.

In the familial excursion, the reflection dives into the custom of narrating evenings — a practice where relatives assemble to share stories, stories, and stories of bygone eras. The faint shine of narrating by candlelight turns into a sacrosanct custom that rises above time, making a space for shared creative mind and holding. The narrating custom turns into a wellspring of bliss as relatives revel in the wealth of shared stories, winding around an aggregate embroidery of recollections that brings chuckling, reflection, and a feeling of coherence.

The investigation goes to the custom of a family excursion — a custom of experience, suddenness, and shared revelation. As the wheels turn and scenes unfurl, the excursion turns out to be in excess of an actual excursion; it turns into a representation for the common way of life. The giggling shared during refueling breaks, the songs reverberating through the vehicle, and the aggregate wonder at beautiful vistas become ceremonies that implant the excursion with satisfaction. The excursion custom turns into a festival of shared investigation, strength, and the delight tracked down in the common excursion.

With regards to familial customs, the reflection explores to the custom of a vacation brightening day. As relatives accumulate to enhance the home with happy decorations, lights, and wreaths, the air is implanted with the soul of bliss and expectation. The cooperative work to change the living space into a happy sanctuary turns into a custom that rises above beautification. It turns into an encapsulation of shared happiness, as each decoration conveys the memory of shared chuckling, inventiveness, and the glow of familial harmony.

Inside the embroidery of strict customs, the reflection investigates the custom of a shared petition or love administration. Whether in the sacrosanct quiet of a basilica or the energetic serenades of a sanctuary, the demonstration of meeting up for aggregate petitioning God turns into a custom that lifts the person to a common profound encounter. The public love custom turns into a channel for a delight that exudes from a common association with the heavenly and a feeling of having a place with a bigger otherworldly local area.

The familial excursion takes a melodic turn in the reflection, zeroing in on the custom of a family chime in night. As the harmonies of old songs consume the space, relatives participate in amicable tune. The chime in custom turns into an upbeat festival of shared melodic recollections, each note reverberating with the reverberations of shared encounters and the glow of familial bonds. Through the force of tune, the family custom turns into a hymn of satisfaction, joining ages in a song that rises above time.

With regards to groundbreaking life altering situations, the reflection goes to the custom of a family inviting service for an infant. The cheerful get-together of family members, the delicate cooing of the baby, and the common gifts become customs that mark the appearance of another life as well as the continuation of familial bonds. The inviting service turns into a glad festival of life, joining relatives in their common jobs as defenders, tutors, and wellsprings of genuine love.

The familial story takes an instructive turn in the reflection, investigating the custom of a family book club. As relatives submerge themselves in shared scholarly universes, the book club turns into a ceremonial space for scholarly trade, smart conversations, and the delight of shared perusing. The turning of pages turns into an aggregate excursion, every part cultivating individual development as well as a common perspective that turns into a wellspring of happiness and scholarly association.

In the domain of outside customs, the reflection goes to the custom of a family setting up camp excursion. The popping of the pit fire, the common warmth of resting under the stars, and the ensemble of nighttime sounds become ceremonies that associate the family to the normal world. The setting up camp outing custom turns into a festival of straightforwardness, versatility, and the common satisfaction tracked down in the basic encounters of nature. Through the glinting flares and stirring leaves, familial bonds are fortified, and a feeling of aggregate marvel is encouraged.

The reflection stretches out to the practice of a family ability show — an occasion where secret abilities and interests become the overwhelming focus. As relatives grandstand their gifts, whether it be singing, moving, or performing enchantment deceives, the ability show turns into a blissful festival of independence and shared appreciation. The spotlight turns into a common space where every part's interesting gifts add to the aggregate satisfaction, cultivating a climate of consolation, support, and shared creative articulation.

With regards to culinary customs, the reflection goes to the custom of a family cooking day. The cleaving of vegetables, the sizzling of flavors, and the cooperative work to make a common dinner become ceremonies that rise above the demonstration of cooking. The family cooking day turns into a festival of flavors, social legacy, and the delight of making something together. Through the common blowout, familial bonds are sustained, and the demonstration of cooking turns into a happy articulation of adoration and harmony.

The investigation of shared customs digs into the practice of a family volunteer day — a formal obligation to rewarding the local area. As relatives participate in aggregate demonstrations of administration, whether through tidying up a neighborhood park or taking part in beneficent drives, the worker day turns into a cheerful articulation of shared values and a promise to having a constructive outcome. Through the common work to make a superior local area, familial bonds are reinforced, and a feeling of mutual perspective is developed.

In the domain of mechanical customs, the reflection investigates the practice of a family film night. The faint sparkle of the screen, the common expectation of a realistic excursion, and the post-film conversations become ceremonies that span ages and make shared social encounters. The film night custom turns into a blissful festival of narrating, chuckling, and the aggregate enthusiasm for true to life craftsmanship. Through the common accounts of film, familial bonds are produced, and the delight found in shared stories is enhanced.

Inside the familial excursion, the reflection goes to the custom of a family legacy trip — a journey to tribal grounds, following the roots that tight spot ages together. As relatives investigate verifiable locales, associate with far off family members, and drench themselves in the social embroidery of their genealogy, the legacy trip turns into a ceremonial festival of character and shared history. Through the common investigation of roots, familial bonds are developed, and a feeling of having a place with a bigger story is insisted.

With regards to celebratory customs, the reflection goes to the custom of a family commemoration festivity. Whether denoting the long stretches of a couple's association or the remembrance of critical family achievements, the commemoration festivity turns into a glad custom of adoration, responsibility, and shared history. The ringing of glasses, the trading of genuine toasts, and the formation of a familial time container become customs that rise above the prompt festival, becoming standards of shared bliss and persevering through responsibility.

The familial story takes an imaginative turn in the reflection, zeroing in on the custom of a family workmanship night. As relatives communicate their thoughts through painting, drawing, or other imaginative undertakings, the workmanship night turns into a ceremonial festival of innovativeness, individual articulation, and shared appreciation. The material turns into a common space where each stroke of the brush adds to an aggregate show-stopper, encouraging a feeling of euphoria tracked down in the demonstration of creation and imaginative joint effort.

With regards to occasional practices, the reflection goes to the custom of a family apple-picking day. The fresh harvest time air, the stirring of leaves, and the aggregate work to cull apples from the branches become ceremonies that associate the family to the patterns of nature. The apple-picking day turns into a blissful festival of the evolving seasons, familial bonds, and the common savor the experience of the abundance of nature. Through the demonstration of gathering, familial associations are braced, and the delight of occasional ceremonies is relished.

The familial excursion takes an otherworldly turn in the reflection, investigating the custom of a family appreciation function. As relatives accumulate to communicate much obliged, whether through verbally expressed words, composed notes, or shared thoughtful gestures, the appreciation function turns into a custom of appreciation, reflection, and shared care. The declaration of appreciation turns into a wellspring of satisfaction that saturates the familial story, encouraging a culture of gratefulness, correspondence, and shared positive energy.

With regards to groundbreaking life minutes, the reflection goes to the practice of a genealogy establishing function. Whether in festival of another life, an achievement, or in memory of a friend or family member, the tree-establishing function turns into a formal certification of life, development, and interconnectedness. The demonstration of planting turns into a common undertaking, a substantial portrayal of familial bonds, and a wellspring of bliss tracked down in the recurrent idea of life.

The investigation of shared ceremonies reaches out to the custom of a family stargazing night. As relatives accumulate under the tremendous field of the night sky, the gleaming stars become a setting for shared marvel, thought, and heavenly investigation. The stargazing night turns into an upbeat custom that rises above natural worries, cultivating a feeling of wonder, solidarity, and shared interest. Through the common look at the universe, familial bonds are reinforced, and the delight of shared thought is engraved in the familial account.

With regards to self-articulation, the reflection goes to the custom of a family verse understanding evening. As relatives share refrains, whether formed by popular writers or made by relatives themselves, the verse perusing night turns into a ceremonial festival of language, feeling, and shared articulation. The sections become a common language, a beautiful embroidery that catches the subtleties of familial connections and turns into a wellspring of euphoria tracked down in the excellence of words.

Inside the familial story, the reflection investigates the custom of a family narrating circle — a deliberate space where every part has the potential chance to share their encounters, dreams, and reflections. The narrating circle turns into a ceremonial festival of individual voices, points of view, and the aggregate insight that rises up out of shared stories. Through the demonstration of tuning in and sharing, familial bonds are fortified, and the delight of public narrating turns into a demonstration of the extravagance of the familial story.

In the domain of celebratory practices, the reflection goes to the custom of a family dance party. Whether in the lounge, patio, or local area corridor, the cadenced beats, shared developments, and uninhibited delight of moving become customs that rise above age, cultivating intergenerational bonds and making shared recollections. The dance party turns into a festival of life, energy, and the sheer enjoyment tracked down in the demonstration of development and shared articulation.

The familial excursion takes an intelligent turn, contemplating the custom of a family appreciation container. As relatives contribute notes of appreciation over time, the appreciation container turns into a formal festival of the little delights, significant minutes, and shared gifts. The demonstration of perusing these notes turns into an aggregate reflection, a wellspring of happiness tracked down in recognizing the overflow of positive encounters inside the familial excursion.

With regards to generational associations, the reflection investigates the custom of a family shrewdness sharing circle. As elderly folks share their life illustrations, encounters, and exhortation, the insight sharing circle turns into a formal festival of intergenerational association and shared learning. The insight shared turns into a wellspring of bliss that rises above individual points of view, cultivating a feeling of progression, regard, and the delight of gaining from each other.

Inside the familial story, the reflection goes to the practice of a family appreciation walk — a common outside movement where relatives express gratitude for the normal magnificence that encompasses them. The appreciation walk turns into a custom of care, reflection, and shared appreciation for their general surroundings.

Chapter 3

"Challenges and Resilience"

"Difficulties and Strength"

In the complicated woven artwork of human life, challenges arise as unavoidable strings, winding through the texture of our lives. The story of difficulties and flexibility unfurls as a significant investigation of the human soul's ability to explore misfortune, adjust to evolving conditions, and arise more grounded. This reflection digs into the horde features of difficulties — individual, cultural, and worldwide — and the inborn versatility that dwells inside people and networks.

The singular excursion through challenges starts in the domain of individual battles, where the story unfurls inside the maze of one's own encounters. In this story, the hero faces the considerable test of beating self-question and leaving on an excursion of self-revelation. The conflict under the surface turns into a pot for self-improvement, flexibility, and the continuous rise of newly discovered strength. The story shows how the showdown of individual difficulties, however laborious, turns into an extraordinary interaction that shapes one's character and produces a steadfast soul.

The investigation of difficulties reaches out to the cultural scene, where the story unfurls with regards to social shameful acts and disparities. Here, people wrestle with the fundamental difficulties installed inside cultural designs. The story turns into a source of inspiration, featuring the versatility of the people who defy and oppose cultural treacheries. Through aggregate developments, backing, and a common obligation to change, networks show strength notwithstanding difficulty, pushing against the flows of disparity to make rushes of positive change.

The story takes a worldwide turn as the account unfurls inside the setting of ecological difficulties. The hero, for this situation, is mankind itself, confronting the outcomes of ecological corruption and environmental change. The test becomes one of aggregate liability and shared strength as networks all over the planet wrestle with the effects of catastrophic events, asset exhaustion, and the earnest requirement for economical practices. The worldwide story highlights the interconnectedness of difficulties and the basic for a unified, versatile reaction to safeguard the planet and secure a reasonable future.

Inside the familial setting, the narrative of difficulties and flexibility flourishes despite unexpected conditions. A family wrestles with the unexpected loss of a friend or family member, exploring the intricate feelings of sorrow and the redefinition of familial jobs. The test turns into a personal one, requiring flexibility at the individual and aggregate levels. The family story turns into a demonstration of the recuperating force of versatility, as individuals support each other, fashion new bonds, and track down strength in their common history.

The investigation of difficulties reaches out to the domain of training, where the story unfurls inside a local area wrestling with the effect of instructive differences. Here, the test is foundational — admittance to quality training is lopsided, and underestimated networks face obstructions to learning. The versatility account arises as instructors, understudies, and backers meet up to address these difficulties. Through creative arrangements, local area commitment, and a resolute obligation to instructive value, the story becomes one of strength chasing information and strengthening.

In the working environment, the story of difficulties and flexibility comes to fruition as people explore the intricacies of expert life. A group faces the test of adjusting to remote work, exploring mechanical obstacles, and keeping a feeling of association. The strength account unfurls as partners track down effective fixes, support each other through the vulnerabilities, and arise with freshly discovered adaptability and versatility. The working environment story turns into an impression of aggregate strength notwithstanding developing work elements.

A familial story of difficulties and flexibility arises inside the setting of wellbeing emergencies. Here, a family faces the conclusion of a persistent sickness, exploring the close to home and down to earth intricacies that go with such difficulties.

The flexibility story unfurls as relatives unite behind their cherished one, search out clinical help, and adjust their day to day routines to oblige the new reality. The familial bonds become a wellspring of solidarity, representing how shared strength can change the story of wellbeing challenges into an account of steadiness and trust.

The story takes a generational turn as the difficulties looked by more seasoned grown-ups come to the front. In this story, old people wrestle with the intricacies of maturing, including medical problems, cultural disengagement, and the variation to changing jobs inside the family. The flexibility story turns into an impression of the insight, versatility, and strength that more established grown-ups bring to their difficulties. Through people group support, intergenerational associations, and a pledge to dynamic maturing, the story becomes one of versatility in later life.

The investigation of difficulties reaches out to the domain of mechanical disturbance, where people and networks go up against the quick development of computerized scenes. The story unfurls as a local area explores the difficulties of a computerized partition, trying to overcome any barrier in admittance to innovation. The strength account arises as local area individuals team up to give computerized education, access, and backing, guaranteeing that all people can take part in the advanced period. The story turns into a demonstration of the strength intrinsic in adjusting to mechanical changes while focusing on inclusivity.

A story of difficulties and strength unfurls with regards to movement, where people and families leave on ventures looking for new open doors. The difficulties of adjusting to another culture, language, and cultural standards become necessary to the migrant experience. The versatility account arises as settlers manufacture associations, fabricate networks, and add to the different embroidered artwork of their embraced homes. The story becomes one of solidarity, versatility, and the extraordinary force of flexibility notwithstanding relocation challenges.

Notwithstanding monetary difficulties, the story unfurls inside a local area exploring the intricacies of employment cutback and monetary flimsiness. The strength story turns into an account of aggregate help, as local area individuals meet up to make work preparing programs, monetary education drives, and common guide organizations. The people group story turns into a demonstration of the flexibility implanted in the aggregate reaction to monetary difficulties, representing how shared endeavors can elevate people and networks.

Inside the domain of emotional wellness, the account of difficulties and flexibility flourishes in the encounters of people confronting mental afflictions. The account unfurls as people stand up to marks of shame, look for help, and explore the intricacies of psychological wellness care. The versatility account turns into an account of individual strength, local area understanding, and the groundbreaking force of psychological wellness support. Through shared encounters, open discourse, and a promise to destigmatizing emotional wellness, the story becomes one of strength notwithstanding mental difficulties.

In the circle of habit recuperation, an account of difficulties and strength arises as people explore the excursion towards restraint. The difficulties of defeating enslavement are diverse, enveloping physical, close to home, and cultural aspects. The flexibility story turns into an impression of the strength found in encouraging groups of people, restorative mediations, and the unflinching obligation to self-awareness. The recuperation story turns into a demonstration of the groundbreaking force of versatility in defeating the difficulties of fixation and modifying an existence of direction and wellbeing.

The story of difficulties and strength reaches out to the worldwide stage, where networks face the mind boggling and interconnected difficulties presented by general wellbeing emergencies. The story unfurls as countries wrestle with the effects of pandemics, organizing worldwide reactions, and adjusting to the quickly changing scene of worldwide wellbeing. The flexibility story turns into an impression of the aggregate endeavors to address worldwide wellbeing challenges, underlining the interconnectedness of countries, the significance of worldwide participation, and the basic for strength notwithstanding shared dangers.

Despite catastrophic events, the account of difficulties and versatility unfurls as networks defy the obliteration created by quakes, tropical storms, fierce blazes, and other devastating occasions. The difficulties are prompt and significant, testing the strength of people, families, and whole locales. The story becomes one of aggregate reaction, as networks meet up to give crisis help, modify foundation, and backing each other in the result of calamity. The story turns into a demonstration of the versatility implanted in human networks, delineating how shared endeavors can modify and reestablish even notwithstanding the most considerable difficulties.

A story of difficulties and versatility unfurls inside the setting of foundational imbalances, where networks wrestle with the persevering through effects of verifiable treacheries. The difficulties are profoundly imbued, traversing ages and sustaining differences in training, work, medical care, and that's just the beginning. The flexibility story turns into an account of fundamental change, as supporters, activists, and networks work energetically to destroy prejudicial frameworks, advocate for equity, and encourage inclusivity. The story turns into an impression of the persevering through strength tracked down in the aggregate quest for value and equity.

In the investigation of difficulties and strength, the story stretches out to the developing scene of relational connections. The difficulties inside connections — be they familial, heartfelt, or dispassionate — become a personal story of development, understanding, and transformation. The flexibility story arises as people and networks explore clashes, develop sympathy, and encourage bonds that endure the everyday hardships. The relational story turns into an impression of the extraordinary force of flexibility in maintaining and fortifying associations.

The overall story of difficulties and versatility turns into an impression of the human ability to adjust, develop, and track down strength even with difficulty.

Whether on an individual, public, or worldwide scale, the story delineates how difficulties are innate to the human experience and how strength, whether found inside people or developed aggregately, turns into the directing power that drives mankind forward. A story praises the dauntless soul, the unflinching obligation to development, and the extraordinary force of versatility that shapes the human story through the recurring pattern of difficulties.

3.1 Discussion of obstacles faced by the family.

"Investigating Family Difficulties: Exploring the Intricate Landscape of Snags"

In the unpredictable snare of familial elements, challenges arise as unavoidable features of the aggregate excursion. The account of day to day life is rich with snapshots of euphoria, shared encounters, and the bonds that integrate ages. Notwithstanding, woven into this embroidery are likewise strings of difficulty, hindrances that test the flexibility of familial bonds and request a nuanced way to deal with route. This conversation digs into the multi-layered hindrances looked by families — going from inner elements to outside pressures — and investigates the systems families utilize to defeat these difficulties, encouraging development, understanding, and the persevering through strength of shared associations.

At the core of familial difficulties lies the intricacy of relational connections. The nuclear family, with its different people molded by extraordinary encounters, points of view, and characters, turns into a pot for understanding and exploring contrasts. Kin contention, a typical test inside families, unfurls as people fight with the regular rivalry for consideration, assets, and parental endorsement. The story becomes one of exchange, as relatives figure out how to offset individual requirements with the aggregate congruity, encouraging flexibility by developing compassion and understanding in the midst of the intrinsic variety inside the family.

As families navigate the excursion of bringing up kids, the test of nurturing styles comes to the front. Different ways to deal with discipline, instruction, and by and large childhood can make pressure inside the familial construction. The story of nurturing difficulties highlights the significance of open correspondence, common regard, and a common obligation to the prosperity of the youngsters. Families explore these deterrents by laying out an underpinning of shared values, taking part in consistent discourse, and adjusting their nurturing methodologies to line up with the developing necessities of their youngsters.

Financial difficulties structure a huge deterrent for some families, impacting their elements, dynamic cycles, and by and large prosperity. Monetary shakiness can strain familial connections as people battle with the stressors of planning, obligation, and financial vulnerabilities. The account of monetary difficulties inside families turns into an account of versatility as individuals team up to explore monetary obstacles. Planning, monetary education, and common help arise as techniques families utilize to climate monetary tempests, stressing the significance of shared liability and fortitude in beating monetary impediments.

With regards to current versatility, geographic scattering turns into an unmistakable test for some families. The story unfurls as individuals wrestle with the effect of movement, be it for vocation valuable open doors, instructive pursuits, or other life conditions. The test lies in keeping familial associations across actual separations. Families utilize different techniques, like customary virtual correspondence, arranged reunions, and purposeful endeavors to remain associated, to connect the geological holes. The story turns into a demonstration of the versatility of familial bonds despite spatial difficulties.

An impactful test inside family stories is the experience of misfortune and sorrow. Whether through the death of a friend or family member, the disintegration of a marriage, or different types of partition, families stand up to the profound intricacies of exploring pain. The account becomes one of aggregate grieving, backing, and flexibility as families rest on each other for strength. Customs of recognition, open correspondence about sentiments, and looking for proficient help add to the mending system, permitting families to explore the difficult landscape of misfortune together.

In the contemporary scene, the unavoidable impact of innovation presents exceptional difficulties to familial elements. The ubiquity of screens, online entertainment, and advanced correspondence presents intricacies like the obscuring of limits among individual and virtual lives. Families explore difficulties connected with screen time, advanced manners, and the effect of innovation on relational connections. The story becomes one of purposeful equilibrium, with families taking on systems to make sans tech zones, assign screen times, and elevate eye to eye cooperations. This continuous exchange features the significance of adjusting relational intricacies to the consistently developing computerized scene.

Social and generational holes present extra layers of challenge inside families, especially in multicultural or multi-generational settings. The account unfurls as relatives wrestle with varying social assumptions, values, and correspondence styles. Generational partitions, set apart by unmistakable points of view molded by various times, make extraordinary difficulties in understanding and associating across age gatherings. Families address these difficulties through undivided attention, encouraging intergenerational exchange, and praising the extravagance that variety brings to the familial embroidery. The story turns into a demonstration of the extraordinary force of embracing contrasts and building spans across social and generational holes.

The moving scene of orientation jobs and assumptions presents its own arrangement of difficulties inside families. The account unfurls as people and families explore developing thoughts of orientation correspondence, shared liabilities, and the destroying of conventional generalizations. Challenges arise in reclassifying jobs, assumptions, and power elements inside familial designs.

The story becomes one of variation, as families take part in open discussions, challenge imbued convictions, and make progress toward a fair circulation of obligations. The excursion toward orientation comprehensive familial elements mirrors the versatility inborn in standing up to and destroying orientation based difficulties.

Wellbeing emergencies, whether ongoing ailments or abrupt health related crises, present imposing difficulties inside family stories. The story unfurls as families explore the profound, monetary, and pragmatic intricacies of medical care. The test lies in adjusting providing care liabilities, adjusting to changes in wellbeing, and supporting each other through clinical difficulties. Families utilize procedures like open correspondence, looking for proficient help, and encouraging a culture of sympathy and support to explore the maze of wellbeing challenges. The story becomes one of aggregate strength, versatility, and a common obligation to the prosperity of every relative.

Inside the domain of instructive difficulties, families wrestle with issues going from scholarly tensions to the advancing scene of schooling. The story unfurls as guardians, understudies, and instructors explore the intricacies of the instructive excursion. Difficulties might incorporate adjusting to remote picking up, tending to learning contrasts, or overseeing scholarly assumptions. Families utilize procedures like open correspondence with teachers, establishing favorable learning conditions at home, and advancing an inspirational perspective toward instruction. The story turns into an impression of shared obligation to learning, versatility, and encouraging a climate that upholds instructive development.

In the circle of habit, families stand up to the imposing test of supporting friends and family through the excursion of recuperation. The story unfurls as families wrestle with the profound cost of fixation, the intricacies of restoration, and the most common way of remaking trust. Difficulties might incorporate tending to empowering ways of behaving, encouraging comprehension, and looking for proficient help. Families explore these impediments through mediations, support gatherings, and a promise to aggregate mending. The story becomes one of strength as families leave on the difficult way toward recuperation together.

The advancing scene of balance between fun and serious activities presents its own arrangement of difficulties inside family accounts. The story unfurls as people endeavor to explore the requests of profession, individual life, and familial obligations. Difficulties might incorporate burnout, time requirements, and the effect of business related weight on familial connections. Families utilize techniques like defining limits, focusing on quality time, and cultivating a culture of common help. The story turns into an impression of the continuous exchange between proficient pursuits and the conservation of familial associations.

Inside the setting of mixed families, the difficulties of exploring complex connections, contrasting nurturing styles, and building union become articulated.

The story unfurls as families wrestle with the complexities of step-nurturing, coordinating different family foundations, and cultivating a feeling of having a place for all individuals. Difficulties might incorporate laying out new practices, tending to clashes, and advancing a feeling of solidarity. Families utilize methodologies like open correspondence, family gatherings, and looking for proficient direction to explore the intricacies of mixed relational peculiarities. The story turns into a demonstration of the flexibility innate in fashioning new bonds and making a durable family character.

The dynamic of family challenges converges with issues connected with psychological well-being, as people inside families stand up to profound and mental difficulties. The story unfurls as families explore the intricacies of emotional wellness conditions, looking for grasping, backing, and pathways to recuperating. Difficulties might incorporate destigmatizing psychological wellness conversations, getting to proper consideration, and encouraging a climate of compassion. Families utilize methodologies like training, correspondence, and aggregate contribution in the excursion toward mental prosperity. The story becomes one of shared strength, versatility, and the groundbreaking force of aggregate help notwithstanding psychological wellness challenges.

The perplexing dance of relational connections inside families additionally brings about the test of correspondence hindrances. The account unfurls as people wrestle with miscommunication, unexpressed sentiments, and the requirement for viable discourse. Difficulties might remember generational contrasts for correspondence styles, language hindrances, or essentially the trouble of communicating feelings. Families address these difficulties through undivided attention, encouraging an open correspondence culture, and looking for proficient direction when required. The story turns into an impression of the groundbreaking force of clear and caring correspondence in exploring familial connections.

A critical test inside family stories is the experience of emergencies, be they cataclysmic events, mishaps, or unexpected crises. The account unfurls as families wrestle with the dire requirement for quick, organized reactions notwithstanding emergency. Difficulties might incorporate the interruption of day to day existence, profound injury, and the requirement for aggregate flexibility. Families utilize methodologies, for example, crisis readiness, local area encouraging groups of people, and the development of an emergency reaction mentality to explore the turbulent territory of startling difficulties. The story becomes one of aggregate strength, flexibility, and a common obligation to enduring emergencies together.

The general story of family challenges is an impression of the complex idea of the familial excursion. Whether the impediments emerge from inside the relational peculiarities or come from outer powers, the story highlights the strength inborn in familial bonds. Families explore the intricate landscape of difficulties through flexibility, open correspondence, common help, and a common obligation to development.

The aggregate story turns into a demonstration of the getting through strength tracked down in familial associations — a strength that faces the hardships of difficulties as well as changes them into potential open doors for mutual perspective, empathy, and the nonstop development of the familial embroidery.

3.2 Examples of how collective strength helps overcome challenges.

"Aggregate Strength: Prevailing Over Difficulties through Solidarity"

The perplexing dance of life frequently faces people and networks with a horde of difficulties. At these times, the force of aggregate strength arises as a reference point of versatility, directing people through difficulty and changing difficulties into potential open doors for development. This investigation digs into different models across assorted settings — going from familial and local area settings to more extensive cultural and worldwide difficulties — where aggregate strength turns into the main thrust that moves people forward, cultivating solidarity, common perspective, and win over snags.

At the core of the familial story, the aggregate strength of relatives surfaces as a strong power in beating difficulties. A strong model unfurls notwithstanding a wellbeing emergency, where a family energizes together to help a part determined to have a constant disease. The aggregate strength becomes obvious in shared providing care liabilities, daily reassurance, and a pledge to keeping a positive climate. As relatives adjust their endeavors and assets, the account changes from one of individual battle to an account of strength, shared love, and the immovable help that drives the family through the difficulties presented by the medical issue.

In the domain of training, the story of aggregate strength unfurls in networks where people meet up to address foundational challenges in the instructive scene. A model surfaces locally endeavoring to connect the advanced gap, guaranteeing that all understudies approach web based learning assets. Through aggregate endeavors, guardians, educators, and local area pioneers team up to give innovation, web network, and instructive help to understudies out of luck. The story becomes one of shared obligation to rise to admittance to training, embodying how aggregate strength destroys boundaries and cultivates a steady climate for scholastic achievement.

Inside people group confronting monetary difficulties, aggregate strength turns into an extraordinary power in the excursion toward monetary dependability. A model arises in a local wrestling with joblessness and monetary strain. Occupants join to make a local area asset focus, extending employment opportunity preparing programs, monetary education studios, and shared help drives. The aggregate strength of the local area drives people toward monetary strengthening, accentuating the force of public help in exploring the intricacies of monetary difficulties. The account shifts from one of individual difficulty to an account of aggregate strength and strengthening.

In the working environment, the account of aggregate strength unfurls as groups meet up to conquer hindrances and accomplish shared objectives. A model surfaces in an organization going through a difficult progress, where workers team up to explore the progressions and guarantee a smooth change. The aggregate strength becomes obvious in open correspondence, shared critical thinking, and a culture of common help. The story changes from one of work environment difficulties to an account of strength, cooperation, and the aggregate exertion that moves the association toward progress.

The investigation of aggregate strength reaches out to the domain of local area building, where occupants join to address shared difficulties and improve the personal satisfaction. A model arises in a local confronting wellbeing concerns, where occupants structure a local area watch program. Through aggregate watchfulness, shared correspondence channels, and a promise to the prosperity of the local area, occupants establish a more secure living climate. The story turns into a demonstration of the groundbreaking force of aggregate strength in encouraging a feeling of safety and solidarity inside the area.

With regards to social and generational holes, the story of aggregate strength comes to fruition as families and networks meet up to connect contrasts and celebrate variety. A model surfaces in a multicultural local area putting together a comprehensive social celebration. Through aggregate endeavors, people from different foundations team up to feature their practices, cooking styles, and workmanship. The story becomes one of solidarity, understanding, and the festival of shared mankind, delineating how aggregate strength destroys social partitions and cultivates a feeling of having a place for all.

The aggregate strength of social developments arises as a powerful power in tending to cultural treacheries and upholding for positive change. A model unfurls in a grassroots development supporting for natural preservation. Activists, people group individuals, and associations join to bring issues to light, hall for strategy changes, and take part in economical practices. The account turns into an account of aggregate strength rising above individual endeavors, showing how a common obligation to a reason can drive groundbreaking change on a cultural level.

The investigation of aggregate strength notwithstanding orientation based difficulties uncovers accounts of strengthening and support. A model surfaces locally endeavoring to take out orientation based separation and advance balance. Through aggregate activism, mindfulness missions, and strategy backing, people join to challenge imbued orientation standards. The story changes from one of orientation based difficulties to an account of aggregate strength destroying foundational disparities and encouraging a more evenhanded society.

With regards to emotional well-being, the story of aggregate strength unfurls as networks cooperate to destigmatize emotional well-being conversations and offer help to those out of luck.

A model arises locally laying out psychological wellness support gatherings, where people share their encounters, offer sympathetic tuning in, and advance mental prosperity. The aggregate strength turns into an encouraging sign, changing the account from one of confinement and disgrace to an account of shared versatility, understanding, and the making of a strong psychological well-being local area.

Inside the domain of fixation recuperation, aggregate strength turns into a foundation of help for people on the way to collectedness. A model surfaces locally coordinating friend support gatherings, where people in recuperation meet up to share their accounts, give consolation, and explore the difficulties of keeping up with restraint. The aggregate strength turns into a life saver, showing how shared encounters and common help can change the account of enslavement into an account of recuperation, development, and versatility.

In the worldwide field, the account of aggregate strength becomes the dominant focal point in resolving major problems, for example, environmental change. A model unfurls in a worldwide alliance of countries teaming up to relieve the effect of ecological corruption. Through aggregate arrangements, shared assets, and a pledge to manageable practices, countries join to address the difficulties presented by environmental change. The account becomes one of worldwide joint effort, accentuating how aggregate strength is fundamental in going up against difficulties that rise above individual lines.

The investigation of aggregate strength inside networks confronting cataclysmic events uncovers stories of fortitude, flexibility, and quick reaction. A model surfaces locally recuperating from a staggering storm, where inhabitants, help associations, and government offices combine efforts to give help, modify framework, and backing those impacted. The account becomes one of shared flexibility, underlining how aggregate strength empowers networks to recuperate and modify in the consequence of cataclysmic events.

Notwithstanding general wellbeing emergencies, the story of aggregate strength arises as networks join to address difficulties presented by pandemics. A model surfaces in a worldwide reaction to a viral flare-up, where countries team up on immunization conveyance, general wellbeing measures, and exploration drives. Through aggregate endeavors, the worldwide local area cooperates to safeguard general wellbeing, showing the groundbreaking force of aggregate strength even with shared difficulties.

Inside the familial setting, aggregate strength turns into a directing power in conquering hindrances going from wellbeing emergencies to generational partitions. A model unfurls in a family exploring the intricacies of providing care for an old part with wellbeing challenges. Relatives meet up, share liabilities, and establish a steady climate. The account becomes one of shared love, versatility, and the groundbreaking force of aggregate strength in exploring familial difficulties.

In the circle of relational connections, the story of aggregate strength comes to fruition as people explore clashes, contrasts, and developing elements. A model surfaces in a close connection confronting difficulties, where accomplices participate in open correspondence, look for directing, and cooperate to reinforce their security. The aggregate strength turns into an impetus for relationship development, representing how shared responsibility and common help can change difficulties into valuable open doors for more profound association.

The all-encompassing story of aggregate strength highlights its groundbreaking power across different settings. Whether inside families, networks, work environments, or worldwide drives, the models outline how shared responsibility, coordinated effort, and common help empower people and gatherings to win over difficulties. The aggregate strength turns into a reference point of versatility, directing humankind through the intricacies of life and outlining that, together, people can accomplish beyond what they might at any point achieve alone.

3.3 Insights into the resilience that comes from mutual support.

"Shared Help: The Foundation of Strength in the Human Excursion"

In the perplexing embroidery of human life, flexibility arises as a characterizing string, woven through the texture of our individual and aggregate stories. At its center, strength mirrors the ability to explore misfortune, bounce back from difficulties, and arise more grounded from life's difficulties. Inside this investigation, the center movements to the groundbreaking force of shared help — a powerful interchange where people, families, and networks draw strength from each other, making a strong embroidery that endures the everyday hardships and situation.

At the core of familial elements, shared help turns into a foundation of versatility, forming the story of families confronting wellbeing challenges. A close knowledge unfurls in the tale of a family exploring a friend or family member's difficult disease. Through the preliminaries of clinical medicines, close to home promising and less promising times, and the re-definition of day to day existence, the relatives find comfort and strength in their common encouraging group of people. The story turns into a demonstration of the flexibility that exudes from shared encounters, shared loads, and the unfaltering help that relatives give to each other.

Inside the setting of instructive difficulties, common help becomes the dominant focal point as understudies, guardians, and teachers meet up to explore the intricacies of the learning venture. An understanding surfaces in the cooperative endeavors of a local area tending to instructive variations. Guardians participate in common encouraging groups of people, sharing assets, information, and consolation to guarantee that all understudies have equivalent open doors for scholarly achievement. The account changes from one of individual battles to an account of aggregate flexibility, showing how common help can connect holes and make an establishment for instructive strengthening.

In the domain of monetary difficulties, shared help turns into a life saver for people and networks wrestling with monetary precariousness. A knowledge arises locally hit hard by employment misfortunes, where neighbors join to make a shared guide organization. Through shared assets, ability sharing, and everyday reassurance, local area individuals explore the vulnerabilities of monetary difficulties. The story becomes one of aggregate versatility, featuring the extraordinary force of shared help in cultivating a feeling of fortitude and strengthening in the midst of monetary difficulties.

In the work environment, shared help turns into an impetus for flexibility as partners combine efforts to explore proficient difficulties. A knowledge surfaces in a group adjusting to remote work, where common help appears as virtual coordinated effort, shared methodologies, and profound consolation. The account changes from individual work environment difficulties to an account of aggregate strength, showing how common help cultivates versatility, group union, and a common obligation to conquering hindrances.

Local area building turns into a material for the extraordinary idea of common help, especially in areas confronting security concerns. An understanding unfurls locally watch program where occupants effectively partake in common encouraging groups of people, cultivating a feeling of shared liability regarding the wellbeing of their area. The story becomes one of aggregate versatility, stressing how common help makes a more secure, more strong local area where people pay special attention to each other.

With regards to social and generational holes, shared help arises as a scaffold that traverses distinctions, encouraging solidarity and understanding. A knowledge surfaces locally arranging social trade occasions, where people from different foundations take part in common help to grandstand and praise their exceptional practices. The story changes from one of social partitions to an account of aggregate versatility, delineating how common help turns into the establishment for building spans across ages and social contrasts.

The aggregate strength of social developments gives a strong illustration of common help on a more extensive cultural scale. A knowledge arises in the account of a promotion bunch attempting to address cultural treacheries, where people join in shared help to enhance their voices and impact change. The story becomes one of aggregate versatility, underscoring how common help inside friendly developments makes a power equipped for testing foundational disparities and driving extraordinary cultural movements.

In the domain of emotional well-being, shared help arises as a key support point for people exploring mental difficulties. An understanding unfurls in the setting of care groups, where people meet up to share their encounters, give sympathetic tuning in, and offer common consolation. The account changes from one of disconnection and disgrace to an account of aggregate strength, showing how common help makes a steady local area that cultivates figuring out, acknowledgment, and the excursion toward mental prosperity.

Inside the setting of compulsion recuperation, common help turns into an encouraging sign for people on the way to restraint. A knowledge surfaces in the tale of recuperation gatherings, where people share their battles, triumphs, and common support. The story becomes one of aggregate versatility, featuring how common help inside recuperation networks assumes a vital part in defeating the difficulties of compulsion and encouraging a feeling of shared strength and reason.

The worldwide reaction to major problems, for example, environmental change, gives a significant knowledge into the extraordinary force of shared help on a planetary scale. A model arises in the cooperative endeavors of countries cooperating to address ecological difficulties. Through shared assets, peaceful accords, and a promise to maintainable practices, countries take part in common help to safeguard the planet. The story becomes one of aggregate versatility, underscoring how shared help on a worldwide level can handle difficulties that rise above individual boundaries.

Notwithstanding catastrophic events, common help turns into a life saver for networks facing the quick fallout and the drawn out recuperation. A knowledge unfurls locally revamping after a staggering storm, where occupants, help associations, and legislatures participate in common help to give crisis help, reconstruct foundation, and backing those impacted. The story becomes one of aggregate strength, representing how common help makes an establishment for local area recuperation and modifying.

General wellbeing emergencies, like pandemics, highlight the basic job of shared help in safeguarding worldwide prosperity. A knowledge arises in the cooperative endeavors of countries, specialists, and medical care experts cooperating to address general wellbeing challenges. Through shared data, clinical assets, and a promise to worldwide participation, common help turns into the key part of a worldwide reaction. The account changes from one of individual countries wrestling with a wellbeing emergency to an account of aggregate versatility, underlining how common help on a worldwide scale is fundamental despite shared dangers to general wellbeing.

Familial stories offer significant bits of knowledge into the versatility that stems from common help. Inside the setting of maturing, common help becomes fundamental for more seasoned grown-ups exploring the intricacies of wellbeing challenges and cultural changes. A knowledge surfaces in a family really focusing on older individuals, where common help appears as shared providing care liabilities, close to home support, and adjusting to developing relational peculiarities. The story becomes one of aggregate flexibility, outlining how common help inside families turns into a wellspring of solidarity, understanding, and shared obligation to the prosperity of more established ages.

In the domain of innovation, where fast changes shape day to day existence, common help becomes pivotal for networks exploring the advanced scene. A knowledge unfurls locally tending to the advanced separation, where people meet up to give innovation access, computerized proficiency support, and shared consolation. The story changes from one of mechanical variations to an account of aggregate flexibility, stressing how common help guarantees that all individuals from the local area can partake in the computerized period.

Common help inside mixed families gives a strong illustration of flexibility even with complex relational elements. An understanding surfaces in the narrative of a mixed family, where shared help turns into the paste that ties different relatives together. Through open correspondence, shared customs, and a pledge to solidarity, the story becomes one of aggregate strength, showing how common help encourages understanding and association in the unpredictable dance of mixed day to day life.

With regards to relocation, common help turns into an imperative power for people and families adjusting to new conditions. A knowledge arises in the story of settlers, where common encouraging groups of people assist novices with exploring social subtleties, lay out local area associations, and fabricate a feeling of having a place. The account changes from one of moves and separation to an account of aggregate flexibility, underscoring how shared help inside worker networks turns into an impetus for fruitful coordination and transformation.

Inside the domain of relational connections, shared help shapes accounts of heartfelt associations confronting difficulties and development. An understanding surfaces in the narrative of a couple exploring the intricacies of a drawn out relationship, where common help turns into the establishment for successful correspondence, shared objectives, and strength notwithstanding challenges. The account changes from one of individual relationship elements to an account of aggregate flexibility, outlining how shared help fortifies the connection between accomplices.

In the circle of maturing, common help turns into an essential part of stories managing end-of-life choices and the intricacies of providing care. A knowledge unfurls in the narrative of a family confronting choices about eldercare, where common help appears as open correspondence, shared liabilities, and profound support. The story becomes one of aggregate strength, stressing how common help inside families turns into a directing power in exploring the many-sided scene of end-of-life care.

In the developing scene of balance between serious and fun activities, shared help becomes fundamental for people endeavoring to orchestrate proficient pursuits and familial obligations. A knowledge surfaces in the story of a functioning guardian, where common encouraging groups of people, adaptable work game plans, and shared childcare obligations become instrumental in exploring the difficulties of adjusting vocation and everyday life.

The account changes from one of individual work-life battles to an account of aggregate versatility, featuring how common help establishes a climate where people can flourish both expertly and by and by.

The investigation of common help inside difficulties connected with emotional wellness offers significant bits of knowledge into the extraordinary force of mutual perspective and sympathy. A model unfurls in the story of people confronting psychological wellness conditions, where common care groups become spaces for shared encounters, support, and destigmatization. The story becomes one of aggregate strength, delineating how common help cultivates a feeling of having a place, diminishes separation, and engages people on their excursion toward mental prosperity.

With regards to enslavement recuperation, common help inside help bunches turns into an encouraging sign for people endeavoring to conquer the difficulties of substance misuse. A knowledge arises in the story of a recuperation local area, where common help appears as shared stories, responsibility, and consolation. The account changes from one of individual battle with dependence on an account of aggregate flexibility, stressing how shared help inside recuperation networks turns into an essential piece of the way to temperance.

The general knowledge got from these different stories is the well known fact that shared help is a principal force in building and supporting strength across different parts of human life. From familial securities to local area fortitude, from work environment elements to worldwide collaboration, common help frames the bedrock of aggregate strength. A unique interaction changes difficulties into potential open doors for development, reinforces associations, and enlightens the common humankind that ties people, families, and networks together on the excursion through life.

The unpredictable dance of common help reaches out into the domain of orientation elements, where the story unfurls despite developing assumptions and difficulties. A knowledge surfaces in networks endeavoring to destroy orientation based generalizations, where shared help turns into a main thrust in pushing for equity. Through shared activism, mindfulness crusades, and the festival of different orientation personalities, people join to challenge imbued standards. The account changes from one of orientation based difficulties to an account of aggregate strength, representing how shared help turns into an impetus for cultural change, encouraging conditions where people can flourish regardless of orientation.

In the unique scene of working environment challenges, common help turns into a core value for groups exploring proficient intricacies. A knowledge unfurls in the tale of a different group tending to working environment stressors, where partners participate in common help through mentorship, cooperative critical thinking, and cultivating a culture of aggregate prosperity.

The account changes from individual profession battles to an account of aggregate versatility, showing how shared help inside the working environment upgrades inventiveness, efficiency, and the general work fulfillment of colleagues.

The investigation of shared help inside social and generational holes gives significant bits of knowledge into accounts where people span partitions to cultivate understanding. A model surfaces in a family exploring social subtleties, where common help turns into an extension between ages, cultivating open correspondence and shared customs. The story becomes one of aggregate flexibility, stressing how shared help inside families destroys social boundaries and makes an agreeable embroidery that mirrors the wealth of different encounters.

With regards to wellbeing emergencies, common help arises as a life saver for networks wrestling with pandemics or broad illnesses. A knowledge unfurls in the worldwide reaction to a wellbeing crisis, where countries participate in common help to share clinical assets, research discoveries, and direction powerful general wellbeing measures. The story changes from individual countries battling a wellbeing emergency to an account of aggregate versatility, outlining how common help on a worldwide scale is basic even with shared dangers to public prosperity.

Cataclysmic events, with their nearby and getting through influence, offer powerful stories where shared help turns into a foundation for local area recuperation. An understanding surfaces locally modifying after a staggering seismic tremor, where occupants, help associations, and legislative bodies take part in shared help to give quick alleviation and work with long haul recuperation. The story becomes one of aggregate flexibility, underscoring how common help makes an establishment for reconstructing and mending in the consequence of catastrophic events.

General wellbeing emergencies, like pandemics, highlight the basic job of common help in safeguarding worldwide prosperity. An understanding arises in the cooperative endeavors of countries, scientists, and medical care experts cooperating to address general wellbeing challenges. Through shared data, clinical assets, and a pledge to worldwide participation, common help turns into the key part of a worldwide reaction. The account changes from one of individual countries wrestling with a wellbeing emergency to an account of aggregate strength, stressing how common help on a worldwide scale is fundamental despite shared dangers to general wellbeing.

In the domain of innovation, where fast changes shape day to day existence, common help becomes pivotal for networks exploring the computerized scene. An understanding unfurls locally tending to the advanced separation, where people meet up to give innovation access, computerized education support, and shared consolation. The account changes from one of mechanical variations to an account of aggregate strength, underscoring how common help guarantees that all individuals from the local area can take part in the computerized period.

Shared help inside mixed families gives a piercing illustration of strength despite complex relational elements. A knowledge surfaces in the tale of a mixed family, where common help turns into the paste that ties different relatives together. Through open correspondence, shared customs, and a pledge to solidarity, the story becomes one of aggregate strength, showing how common help cultivates understanding and association in the unpredictable dance of mixed day to day life.

With regards to movement, shared help turns into an essential power for people and families adjusting to new conditions. An understanding arises in the story of settlers, where shared encouraging groups of people assist rookies with exploring social subtleties, lay out local area associations, and fabricate a feeling of having a place. The story changes from one of moves and disengagement to an account of aggregate strength, stressing how shared help inside outsider networks turns into an impetus for effective coordination and variation.

Inside the domain of relational connections, shared help shapes stories of heartfelt organizations confronting difficulties and development. A knowledge surfaces in the tale of a couple exploring the intricacies of a drawn out relationship, where common help turns into the establishment for viable correspondence, shared objectives, and flexibility even with difficulties. The story changes from one of individual relationship elements to an account of aggregate versatility, showing how common help fortifies the connection between accomplices.

In the circle of maturing, shared help turns into a critical part of stories managing end-of-life choices and the intricacies of providing care. An understanding unfurls in the narrative of a family confronting choices about eldercare, where common help appears as open correspondence, shared liabilities, and profound consolation. The story becomes one of aggregate strength, stressing how common help inside families turns into a directing power in exploring the mind boggling scene of end-of-life care.

In the advancing scene of balance between serious and fun activities, common help becomes fundamental for people endeavoring to blend proficient pursuits and familial obligations. An understanding surfaces in the story of a functioning guardian, where common encouraging groups of people, adaptable work plans, and shared childcare obligations become instrumental in exploring the difficulties of adjusting vocation and everyday life. The story changes from one of individual work-life battles to an account of aggregate flexibility, featuring how common help establishes a climate where people can flourish both expertly and by and by.

The investigation of common help inside difficulties connected with psychological wellness offers significant experiences into the extraordinary force of mutual perspective and compassion. A model unfurls in the story of people confronting emotional well-being conditions, where common care groups become spaces for shared encounters, support, and destigmatization.

The story becomes one of aggregate strength, showing how shared help encourages a feeling of having a place, lessens confinement, and enables people on their excursion toward mental prosperity.

With regards to compulsion recuperation, common help inside help bunches turns into an encouraging sign for people endeavoring to conquer the difficulties of substance misuse. An understanding arises in the story of a recuperation local area, where common help appears as shared stories, responsibility, and consolation. The story changes from one of individual battle with dependence on an account of aggregate flexibility, underlining how common help inside recuperation networks turns into a fundamental piece of the way to balance.

The general knowledge got from these different stories is the well known fact that common help is a major power in building and supporting versatility across different parts of human life. From familial securities to local area fortitude, from working environment elements to worldwide collaboration, shared help frames the bedrock of aggregate strength. A unique transaction changes difficulties into open doors for development, reinforces associations, and enlightens the common mankind that ties people, families, and networks together on the excursion through life.

Chapter 4

"Responsibilities and Roles"

"Obligations and Jobs: The Developing Elements in Human Associations"

In the mind boggling embroidery of human connections, obligations and jobs structure the twist and weft, winding around the account of shared associations. This investigation digs into the diverse elements of obligations and jobs, following their development across familial, cultural, and individual scenes. From the elements inside nuclear families to the more extensive cultural assumptions, the interchange of liabilities and jobs shapes the forms of human associations, mirroring the nuanced and always changing nature of our aggregate process.

At the core of the familial story, obligations and jobs unfurl in a perplexing dance that characterizes the construction of nuclear families. Inside the customary family system, predefined jobs frequently depict the obligations of every part. Guardians expect jobs as suppliers and nurturers, while youngsters explore the jobs of students and wards. The account mirrors the innate relationship inside families, with every part adding to the aggregate prosperity. As cultural standards shift, nonetheless, the customary jobs go through change, bringing about additional liquid and evenhanded elements where obligations are shared, and jobs are re-imagined.

With regards to providing care liabilities, a piercing story arises as families explore the difficulties of giving consideration to old individuals. Customarily, the job of providing care has frequently fallen on grown-up youngsters, especially little girls, reflecting cultural assumptions and social standards. In any case, as the scene of familial obligations develops, a more populist approach arises. Life partners, kin, and more distant family individuals effectively take part in providing care, reshaping the story to one of shared liabilities and cooperative jobs. The advancing elements highlight the flexibility inborn in families as they explore the intricacies of maturing and providing care.

The account of orientation jobs inside families meets with more extensive cultural assumptions, revealing insight into the advancing elements of obligations. In customary systems, orientation jobs have frequently been recommended, with men as essential providers and ladies as overseers. Nonetheless, cultural movements and the quest for orientation equity have prompted a reexamination of these jobs. The account unfurls as families challenge orientation standards, with the two accomplices effectively taking part in proficient pursuits, childcare, and family obligations. The developing jobs mirror a takeoff from conventional assumptions, underscoring a more adjusted circulation of obligations inside familial units.

The investigation reaches out to the domain of nurturing liabilities, where cultural assumptions and individual decisions converge. The story unfurls as guardians explore the fragile harmony among work and everyday life. Conventional jobs cast fathers basically as suppliers and moms as essential parental figures. Notwithstanding, developing cultural standards and changing assumptions rethink nurturing jobs. Fathers effectively participate in involved nurturing, testing generalizations and adding to a story that underlines shared liabilities in bringing up youngsters. The advancing elements highlight the extraordinary force of splitting away from inflexible job assumptions inside the nuclear family.

Cultural assumptions assume a huge part in forming the story of obligations and jobs, especially inside the more extensive local area. The customary jobs doled out in light of cultural designs frequently accompany certain assumptions, impacting people's way of behaving and forming their commitments to the system. In proficient settings, orientation jobs have generally impacted vocation decisions and headway valuable open doors. The story unfurls as people challenge these assumptions, with developments pushing for orientation balance and separating obstructions that limit amazing open doors in view of predefined jobs.

The story of cultural obligations stretches out to the more extensive setting of local area commitment and metro obligations. As individuals from a general public, people are many times relegated jobs that add to the prosperity of the local area. Whether through humanitarian effort, city support, or local area administration, the story mirrors a feeling of shared liability regarding the aggregate government assistance. The developing elements challenge customary thoughts of latent jobs inside society, empowering people to effectively partake in molding their networks and adding to positive social change.

The investigation of obligations and jobs inside the work environment uncovers stories molded by proficient assumptions and authoritative designs. Customarily, work environment jobs have frequently been characterized by various leveled structures, with unmistakable obligations allocated in light of occupation titles. The account unfurls as associations adjust to additional comprehensive and cooperative models, testing inflexible job assumptions. Adaptable work game plans, cooperative direction, and an emphasis on representative prosperity become necessary parts of the developing working environment story. The elements mirror a takeoff from customary ordered progressions, underlining a more libertarian approach that values individual commitments and shared liabilities.

The story of influential positions inside associations gives experiences into the advancing elements of obligations and assumptions. Customary influential positions frequently stuck to progressive designs, with a hierarchical way to deal with navigation. Nonetheless, the account shifts as associations embrace comprehensive initiative models that focus on coordinated effort and different viewpoints. Pioneers are progressively expected to encourage a comprehensive culture, advance variety, and explore complex difficulties cooperatively. The developing elements highlight a takeoff from dictator initiative styles, underlining shared liabilities in controlling associations toward progress.

With regards to cultural assumptions, the story of providing care liabilities meets with orientation jobs, introducing a nuanced investigation of familial elements. Generally, providing care jobs have been overwhelmingly doled out to ladies, reflecting cultural standards and assumptions. The story unfurls as families challenge these customary jobs, with men effectively partaking in providing care liabilities. The developing elements mirror a takeoff from orientation based assumptions, stressing the significance of shared liabilities in giving consideration to relatives.

The investigation of jobs inside the instructive scene divulges stories that highlight the extraordinary force of mentorship and shared liabilities. Customarily, teachers assumed characterized parts inside the homeroom, granting information and direction to understudies. The story unfurls as instructive models shift to embrace cooperative learning conditions, where teachers and understudies effectively take part in the co-production of information. Mentorship turns into a foundation of the story, underscoring shared liabilities in encouraging the development and improvement of students.

In the story of cultural assumptions, obligations and jobs converge with the developing elements of variety and consideration. Customarily, cultural jobs frequently reflected homogenous assumptions, with restricted acknowledgment of different characters and encounters. The story unfurls as social orders embrace inclusivity, testing predefined jobs and assumptions. The acknowledgment of assorted viewpoints becomes fundamental to the story, accentuating shared liabilities in establishing conditions that celebrate contrasts and advance value.

The investigation of obligations and jobs inside familial elements stretches out to the complicated territory of mixed families. The account unfurls as people explore the complexities of step-nurturing, co-nurturing, and incorporating different family foundations. Generally, jobs inside mixed families might have been testing, reflecting cultural assumptions and likely struggles. The developing elements stress open correspondence, adaptability, and shared liabilities, cultivating a story of solidarity and grasping inside mixed nuclear families.

With regards to maturing, the story of obligations and jobs unfurls as families explore the intricacies of eldercare. Generally, the obligation of really focusing on old relatives frequently fell on grown-up kids, reflecting cultural standards. The story changes as families take on cooperative ways to deal with eldercare, with kin, more distant family individuals, and expert guardians effectively partaking in shared liabilities. The developing elements highlight the significance of correspondence, sympathy, and shared responsibilities in giving consideration to maturing relatives.

Inside the domain of emotional well-being, the account of liabilities and jobs mirrors the developing elements of destigmatization and backing. Customarily, cultural assumptions might have projected emotional wellness challenges in a sorry excuse for quietness and separation. The story unfurls as people challenge these assumptions, pushing for open discussions, sympathy, and shared liabilities in supporting mental prosperity. The developing elements stress the extraordinary force of aggregate comprehension and shared liabilities in encouraging conditions that focus on emotional wellness.

With regards to fixation recuperation, obligations and jobs assume a crucial part in forming stories of help and versatility. Customarily, cultural impression of enslavement might have defamed people, restricting open doors for recuperation and reintegration. The story changes as social orders embrace a more merciful methodology, perceiving dependence as a wellbeing challenge as opposed to an ethical coming up short. Shared liabilities inside networks, encouraging groups of people, and medical care frameworks become essential to the account, cultivating conditions that focus on recuperation, understanding, and shared help.

The general understanding got from these different accounts is the well known fact that obligations and jobs are not static; rather, they are dynamic, developing substances that shape and are formed by cultural standards, individual decisions, and aggregate assumptions. The accounts investigated range the familial, cultural, instructive, and proficient circles, revealing a rich embroidery of interconnected stories. From provoking conventional orientation jobs to rethinking authority in associations, the advancing elements underscore the groundbreaking force of shared liabilities in encouraging more comprehensive, fair, and empathetic human associations. As obligations and jobs keep on advancing, the account mirrors a continuous excursion of variation, sympathy, and aggregate development in the complex dance of human connections.

4.1 Exploration of individual roles within the family.

"Investigation of Individual Jobs Inside the Family: Exploring Elements, Obligations, and Bonds"

In the mind boggling embroidery of familial connections, the investigation of individual jobs divulges a nuanced story that shapes the elements, obligations, and bonds inside the nuclear family. Every part contributes an extraordinary string to the texture of the family, winding around an aggregate story of shared encounters, development, and interconnectedness. This investigation digs into the advancing idea of individual jobs inside the family, navigating conventional assumptions, contemporary movements, and the perplexing exchange of liabilities that characterize the family scene.

Customarily, the family structure frequently stuck to predefined jobs, where fathers were the essential providers and moms were the essential parental figures. Youngsters, thus, explored jobs as students and wards. While these customary jobs might have given a feeling of request and dependability, cultural movements have led to a more liquid and evenhanded methodology. The story unfurls as families challenge these customary assumptions, embracing a variety of jobs that mirror the developing elements of current life.

The job of guardians inside the family fills in as a primary support point in forming the story of individual obligations. Customarily, fathers were entrusted with giving monetary steadiness, while moms expected the essential providing care job. Be that as it may, contemporary families witness a takeoff from these unbending assumptions, as the two guardians effectively partake in different parts of day to day life. The story changes to one of shared liabilities, underlining a cooperative way to deal with nurturing that sustains close to home associations, shared navigation, and a more impartial dispersion of errands.

The developing elements of nurturing jobs meet with the account of orientation equity, reflecting more extensive cultural movements. The customary thought that specific obligations are innately attached to orientation has gone through change, and families effectively challenge these assumptions. Fathers take part in sustaining and providing care, splitting away from generalizations, while moms seek after vocations and add to the family's monetary prosperity. The account unfurls as families rethink nurturing jobs, cultivating a climate where individual qualities are commended, and obligations are shared in view of capacities as opposed to orientation standards.

The story reaches out to the job of youngsters inside the family, enlightening the advancing elements of their obligations and commitments. Generally saw as wards, youngsters are progressively perceived as dynamic members in significantly shaping everyday life. As schooling and mindfulness rise, youngsters' jobs extend past the bounds of conventional assumptions.

They become supporters of dynamic cycles, offer remarkable viewpoints, and effectively take part in shared liabilities, encouraging a story of cooperation that sets them up for a future where individual organization is esteemed.

Kin elements assume an essential part in molding the story of individual jobs inside the family. Customarily, kin might have been relegated explicit jobs in view of birth request, with more established kin expecting positions of authority and more youthful ones as supporters. Nonetheless, the account unfurls as families perceive and praise the uniqueness of every kin, taking into consideration the improvement of individual characters. Kin effectively participate in shared liabilities, support each other's development, and add to the general prosperity of the nuclear family.

The investigation of individual jobs inside the family reaches out to the elements of more distant family individuals, featuring the interconnected trap of connections. Grandparents, aunties, uncles, and cousins each contribute particular strings to the familial embroidery. Customarily, these jobs might have been barely characterized, with grandparents filling in as tutors and aunties/uncles giving direction. Nonetheless, the story changes as families perceive the different qualities and commitments of more distant family individuals. They become indispensable mainstays of help, offering a rich embroidery of encounters, shrewdness, and shared liabilities that upgrade the family's versatility and network.

The account of individual jobs inside the family unfurls against the background of social and cultural assumptions, mirroring the more extensive setting where familial connections are arranged. Social standards might impact explicit assumptions about the jobs of seniors, the obligations of grown-up youngsters, and the elements of intergenerational connections. The story turns into a complex dance among custom and advancement, as families explore the fragile equilibrium of saving social qualities while embracing contemporary changes in individual jobs.

With regards to maturing, the story of individual jobs inside the family takes on a novel tint as families explore the intricacies of eldercare. Generally, the obligation of really focusing on maturing guardians frequently falls on grown-up kids, especially girls. Be that as it may, the developing elements mirror a takeoff from customary assumptions, as families embrace cooperative ways to deal with eldercare. Grown-up kin effectively take part in shared liabilities, drawing on different qualities and assets to give all encompassing consideration to maturing relatives. The account highlights the significance of correspondence, sympathy, and shared responsibilities in exploring the complicated scene of eldercare.

The investigation of individual jobs inside the family unfurls with regards to familial emergencies, featuring the extraordinary force of flexibility and shared liabilities. Whether confronting monetary difficulties, wellbeing emergencies, or inner disturbances, families explore these tempests through an aggregate exertion.

The account changes as relatives rally together, drawing on individual qualities and offering shared help. Shared liabilities become a signal of strength, enlightening the way through misfortune and supporting the bonds that characterize the nuclear family.

The account of individual jobs inside the family reaches out to the domain of dynamic cycles, mirroring the elements of force, authority, and shared liabilities. Customarily, direction might have been concentrated, with a patriarch or matron expecting a prevailing job. Nonetheless, contemporary families witness a shift toward cooperative independent direction, where every part's voice is esteemed, and obligations are shared. The story changes into one of inclusivity, underscoring the significance of open correspondence, dynamic cooperation, and aggregate dynamic in encouraging an amicable family climate.

The account of individual jobs inside the family meets with the idea of profound work, featuring the frequently concealed and underestimated liabilities that add to the family's personal prosperity. Close to home work envelops the administration of feelings, the arrangement of help, and the development of good familial associations. Generally, close to home work might have been doled out more to ladies inside the family, reflecting cultural assumptions. Nonetheless, the developing story perceives the significance of shared close to home work, where all relatives effectively add to establishing a sustaining and steady profound climate.

Individual jobs inside the family stretch out to the domain of familial ceremonies and customs, forming the account of shared encounters and social personality. Customarily, certain jobs might have been alloted in light of orientation or age during social functions or familial festivals. The story changes as families embrace a more comprehensive way to deal with these ceremonies, permitting every part to take part and add to the conservation of social legacy effectively. Shared liabilities in keeping up with familial practices become a wellspring of association, encouraging a feeling of progression and character across ages.

The investigation of individual jobs inside the family unfurls with regards to innovation and its effect on familial elements. In the computerized age, jobs might advance to incorporate liabilities connected with innovation use, for example, overseeing on the web correspondence, directing relatives through the computerized scene, and encouraging mindful internet based conduct. The story mirrors a powerful exchange between conventional familial jobs and the incorporation of innovation, underscoring the significance of adjusting to changing scenes while safeguarding the pith of familial associations.

The story of individual jobs inside the family interweaves with the idea of independence and freedom, especially as kids change into adulthood. Customarily, the shift from reliance to freedom denoted a critical achievement, with grown-up youngsters expecting more independent jobs.

Notwithstanding, the advancing story perceives the significance of reliance, where grown-up kids keep up with close associations with their families while seeking after individual objectives and goals. Shared liabilities in supporting each other's processes become fundamental to the story of familial securities that rise above conventional ideas of autonomy.

The investigation of individual jobs inside the family stretches out to the domain of monetary obligations and monetary commitments. Generally, the job of the provider might have been all the more barely characterized, with an essential spotlight on monetary arrangement. The story changes as families perceive the different manners by which people can add to the family's financial prosperity. Shared liabilities in monetary preparation, planning, and cooperative dynamic become fundamental parts of the account, mirroring the changing scene of familial jobs in financial settings.

The story of individual jobs inside the family unfurls with regards to worldwide portability and multicultural encounters. In an undeniably interconnected world, families might explore different social foundations, dialects, and customs. The account turns into an investigation of social combination, where people effectively add to the blend of assorted social components inside the family. Shared liabilities in protecting social character, cultivating multifaceted comprehension, and exploring the intricacies of multicultural encounters become fundamental to the account of globalized familial elements.

The investigation of individual jobs inside the family interweaves with the idea of psychological well-being and close to home prosperity. Customarily, conversations around psychological wellness might have been covered peacefully and shame. The story changes as families effectively take part in discussions about emotional wellness, perceiving the significance of shared liabilities in establishing a strong and compassionate climate. Individual jobs stretch out to the arrangement of consistent reassurance, undivided attention, and cooperative endeavors to focus on mental prosperity inside the family.

With regards to instruction, the story of individual jobs inside the family mirrors the significance of encouraging a steady learning climate. Generally, guardians might have been viewed as essential instructors, directing youngsters through scholarly pursuits. The story changes as families perceive the common obligations in establishing a comprehensive learning climate that stretches out past proper schooling. Kin, grandparents, and more distant family individuals effectively add to the instructive story, offering different points of view and improving the growth opportunity.

The story of individual jobs inside the family unfurls with regards to festivities and achievements, denoting the sections of life. Customarily, certain jobs might have been appointed in light of social or familial assumptions during weddings, birthday celebrations, and other huge occasions.

The story changes as families embrace a more customized and comprehensive way to deal with festivities, permitting every part to take an interest and add to the euphoric minutes effectively. Shared liabilities in arranging and executing festivities become a wellspring of aggregate satisfaction, building up the bonds that characterize the nuclear family.

The investigation of individual jobs inside the family stretches out to the domain of wellbeing and health, mirroring the interconnected idea of familial prosperity. Generally, certain jobs might have been appointed in view of orientation or mature in issues of medical care and health. The story changes as families embrace a more comprehensive methodology, perceiving the common obligations in advancing wellbeing and prosperity for all individuals. Cooperative endeavors in taking on sound ways of life, encouraging preventive consideration, and supporting each other's prosperity become vital parts of the story.

The story of individual jobs inside the family meets with the idea of strength, especially despite difficulties and emergencies. Families explore misfortune through an aggregate exertion, drawing on individual qualities and shared liabilities. The account changes into an account of versatility, where relatives support each other through challenges, cultivate open correspondence, and effectively participate in critical thinking. Shared liabilities become a wellspring of solidarity, empowering families to defeat obstructions and arise more grounded together.

The investigation of individual jobs inside the family uncovers a dynamic and developing story that reflects the intricacies of current life. From provoking customary orientation standards to reclassifying nurturing jobs, from exploring maturing and eldercare to embracing assorted social encounters, the story mirrors the strength, flexibility, and interconnectedness that characterize familial connections. Shared liabilities arise as an ongoing idea, winding around the nuclear family together and cultivating a feeling of aggregate reason. As families keep on exploring the consistently changing scene of cultural assumptions and individual goals, the investigation of individual jobs inside the family stays a continuous excursion of development, understanding, and the festival of the special commitments every part brings to the familial embroidery.

4.2 How each member contributes to the collective strength.

"How Every Part Adds to the Aggregate Strength of the Family: An Embroidery of Shared Liabilities, Backing, and Versatility"

In the unpredictable dance of familial connections, the aggregate strength of a family is woven together by the special commitments of every part. The story unfurls as an embroidery of shared liabilities, common help, and versatility, featuring the manners by which individual qualities and commitments interlace to make a strong and interconnected nuclear family. This investigation dives into the jobs of every relative, explaining the powerful transaction that cultivates a feeling of solidarity and courage inside the family.

Guardians, as the essential mainstays of the family structure, assume urgent parts in molding the aggregate strength. Generally, fathers might have been viewed as suppliers, guaranteeing monetary strength and security for the family. In any case, the story changes as contemporary dads effectively take part in providing care, basic encouragement, and the sustaining of familial bonds. Their commitments stretch out past the conventional supplier job, encouraging a climate where shared liabilities become basic to the family's solidarity.

Moms, frequently thought to be the core of the family, bring a horde of commitments that structure the profound and sustaining center. Generally connected with providing care, moms explore the mind boggling territory of bringing up kids, overseeing family obligations, and offering profound help. The account changes as present day moms offset these jobs with pursuits outside the home, adding to the family's aggregate strength through different abilities and abilities. Their versatility and flexibility become urgent strings in the familial embroidered artwork.

Youngsters, the blooming buds inside the family, add to the aggregate strength through their one of a kind points of view, energy, and development. Generally saw as wards, the story advances as kids effectively participate in the relational peculiarities', offering new experiences, satisfaction, and a mixture of imperativeness. As students, they add to the family's common encounters, while their independence turns into a wellspring of enhancement, significantly shaping the family's personality and cultivating a feeling of coherence.

Kin, limited by shared encounters and familial ties, assume particular parts in adding to the aggregate strength. Customarily seen through birth request elements, the account changes as kin effectively take part in common help, friendship, and the route of life's difficulties together. The bonds fashioned among kin become vital strings in the familial embroidery, adding to a feeling of solidarity, understanding, and shared strength.

More distant family individuals, including grandparents, aunties, uncles, and cousins, add layers of wealth to the familial story. Customarily alloted jobs as coaches or guides, the story develops as more distant family individuals effectively add to the family's aggregate strength. Grandparents offer insight and experience, aunties and uncles become wellsprings of help and direction, and cousins add to the common recollections and brotherhood. The interconnected trap of more distant family connections winds around extra strings of strength and interconnectedness.

With regards to maturing, senior relatives bring an abundance of involvement and understanding that turns into a wellspring of solidarity for the whole family. Generally, the obligation of really focusing on maturing guardians might have fallen on grown-up youngsters, yet the story changes as families take on cooperative ways to deal with eldercare. Shared liabilities in offering close to home help, going with medical care choices, and guaranteeing an honorable and open to maturing process add to the family's general strength.

The account stretches out to the assorted jobs inside mixed families, where stepparents, step-kin, and half-kin add to the familial woven artwork. Generally, these jobs might have been trying because of cultural assumptions and possible contentions. Be that as it may, the account changes as open correspondence, adaptability, and shared liabilities become the establishment for solidarity and grasping inside mixed nuclear families. Every part's exceptional commitments cultivate a climate of inclusivity and aggregate strength.

The advancing elements of individual jobs inside the family converge with social and cultural assumptions, mirroring the more extensive setting wherein familial connections are arranged. Social standards might impact explicit assumptions about the jobs of elderly folks, the obligations of grown-up youngsters, and the elements of intergenerational connections. The account turns into a mind boggling dance among custom and advancement, as families explore the fragile equilibrium of protecting social qualities while embracing contemporary changes in individual jobs.

With regards to familial emergencies, the aggregate strength of the family is exemplified through the manners by which every part adds to conquering difficulties. Whether confronting monetary difficulties, well-being emergencies, or inner disturbances, the story changes into an account of flexibility as relatives rally together. Shared liabilities in critical thinking, consistent reassurance, and exploring affliction become essential parts of the family's aggregate strength.

The account of aggregate strength entwines with the idea of dynamic cycles inside the family. Customarily, direction might have been concentrated, with a patriarch or matron expecting a predominant job. Nonetheless, the story changes as families embrace cooperative direction, where every part's voice is esteemed, and obligations are shared. The inclusivity in dynamic encourages a feeling of solidarity, strengthening, and shared liability in controlling the family toward aggregate prosperity.

Profound work, frequently concealed and underestimated, contributes essentially to the family's aggregate strength. Close to home work incorporates the administration of feelings, the arrangement of help, and the development of good familial associations. Customarily, close to home work might have been allocated more to ladies inside the family, reflecting cultural assumptions. Notwithstanding, the developing story perceives the significance of shared profound work, where all relatives effectively add to establishing a sustaining and steady close to home climate.

The story of individual commitments reaches out to the monetary obligations and monetary commitments inside the family. Customarily, the job of the provider might have been all the more barely characterized, with an essential spotlight on monetary arrangement. The story changes as families perceive the different manners by which people can add to the family's monetary prosperity.

Shared liabilities in monetary preparation, planning, and cooperative dynamic become fundamental parts of the story, mirroring the changing scene of familial jobs in financial settings.

The account of individual commitments inside the family unfurls with regards to worldwide versatility and multicultural encounters. In an undeniably interconnected world, families might explore different social foundations, dialects, and customs. The account turns into an investigation of social combination, where people effectively add to the amalgamation of different social components inside the family. Shared liabilities in safeguarding social character, cultivating multifaceted comprehension, and exploring the intricacies of multicultural encounters become necessary to the account of globalized familial elements.

The investigation of individual commitments interlaces with the idea of independence and freedom, especially as kids change into adulthood. Generally, the shift from reliance to freedom denoted a critical achievement, with grown-up kids expecting more independent jobs. Be that as it may, the developing account perceives the significance of reliance, where grown-up kids keep up with close associations with their families while chasing after individual objectives and yearnings. Shared liabilities in supporting each other's processes become basic to the account of familial bonds that rise above customary ideas of autonomy.

Innovation and its effect on familial elements acquaint new aspects with individual commitments inside the family. In the computerized age, jobs might advance to incorporate liabilities connected with innovation use, for example, overseeing on the web correspondence, directing relatives through the computerized scene, and encouraging mindful web-based conduct. The story mirrors a powerful transaction between conventional familial jobs and the incorporation of innovation, underscoring the significance of adjusting to changing scenes while saving the quintessence of familial associations.

Emotional wellness and close to home prosperity are essential parts of the story of individual commitments inside the family. Customarily, conversations around emotional wellness might have been covered peacefully and disgrace. The story changes as families effectively take part in discussions about emotional well-being, perceiving the significance of shared liabilities in establishing a steady and compassionate climate. Individual jobs stretch out to the arrangement of daily encouragement, undivided attention, and cooperative endeavors to focus on mental prosperity inside the family.

With regards to instruction, individual commitments inside the family mirror the significance of encouraging a strong learning climate. Customarily, guardians might have been viewed as essential teachers, directing kids through scholastic pursuits. The story changes as families perceive the common obligations in establishing a comprehensive learning climate that stretches out past conventional schooling. Kin, grandparents, and more distant family individuals effectively add to the instructive account, offering assorted viewpoints and enhancing the opportunity for growth.

The story of individual commitments inside the family unfurls with regards to festivities and achievements, denoting the entries of life. Customarily, certain jobs might have been alloted in light of social or familial assumptions during weddings, birthday celebrations, and other critical occasions. The story changes as families embrace a more customized and comprehensive way to deal with festivities, permitting every part to take part and add to the euphoric minutes effectively. Shared liabilities in arranging and executing festivities become a wellspring of aggregate satisfaction, building up the bonds that characterize the nuclear family.

Wellbeing and health are principal parts of individual commitments inside the family. Customarily, certain jobs might have been alloted in light of orientation or progress in years in issues of medical services and health. The story changes as families take on a more comprehensive methodology, perceiving the common obligations in advancing wellbeing and prosperity for all individuals. Cooperative endeavors in taking on sound ways of life, cultivating preventive consideration, and supporting each other's prosperity become essential parts of the story.

The story of individual commitments inside the family crosses with the idea of versatility, especially despite difficulties and emergencies. Families explore misfortune through an aggregate exertion, drawing on individual qualities and shared liabilities. The story changes into an account of strength, where relatives support each other through challenges, cultivate open correspondence, and effectively participate in critical thinking. Shared liabilities become a wellspring of solidarity, empowering families to defeat snags and arise more grounded together.

The investigation of how every part adds to the aggregate strength of the family illustrates interconnectedness, common help, and shared flexibility. From guardians molding the establishment to kids implanting essentialness, from more distant family individuals enhancing the embroidery to exploring the intricacies of globalized encounters, every individual's commitments become vital strings in the familial account. As families keep on adjusting to evolving scenes, embrace inclusivity, and encourage open correspondence, the aggregate strength flourishes, making a strong and interconnected familial embroidery that endures the everyday hardships.

4.3 Balancing responsibilities and fostering a sense of shared duty.

"Adjusting Liabilities and Encouraging a Feeling of Shared Obligation: The Agreeable Dance of Relational peculiarities"

In the unpredictable embroidery of familial connections, the fragile harmony between obligations and the development of a common feeling of obligation structure the establishment for amicable relational peculiarities. This investigation dives into the craft of adjusting individual commitments, supporting a cooperative soul, and encouraging an aggregate responsibility that winds around together the strings of shared obligation inside the nuclear family.

Customarily, family obligations have been portrayed along orientation and generational lines, with unmistakable jobs appointed to every part. Fathers were in many cases the essential providers, while moms bore the obligations of providing care and homemaking. As cultural standards develop, the story changes, testing conventional assumptions and preparing for a more evenhanded conveyance of obligations. Adjusting these jobs turns into a nuanced dance, as families explore the changing scenes of orientation elements and reclassify the conventional divisions of work.

The excursion of adjusting liabilities reaches out to nurturing jobs, where the fragile exchange among directing and supporting shapes the family account. Generally, moms were in many cases seen as the essential parental figures, offering close to home help and regulating the everyday requirements of the kids. The account develops as fathers effectively take part in nurturing, adding to navigation, and cultivating close to home associations. Adjusting the requests of vocation and nurturing turns into a common obligation, underscoring the significance of cooperative nurturing in shaping the family's aggregate strength.

The developing elements of obligations cross with the difficulties and delights of bringing up kids inside a contemporary system. The story unfurls as families explore the intricacies of schooling, extracurricular exercises, and the consistently present job of innovation in youngsters' lives. Adjusting the requirement for design and discipline with the support of freedom and inventiveness turns into a common obligation, mirroring the family's obligation to giving a sustaining climate to the comprehensive improvement of every kid.

Kin, limited by the ties of familial love, add to the story of shared obligation through their connections, backing, and understanding. Generally, kin elements might have been affected by birth request, with more established kin taking on influential positions and more youthful ones sticking to this same pattern. The story changes as families perceive and commend the uniqueness of every kin, encouraging a feeling of shared liability in the excursion of development and self-disclosure. Adjusting the elements of kin connections includes developing compassion, open correspondence, and a shared obligation to one another's prosperity.

The account reaches out to the domain of more distant family individuals, where the elements of adjusting liabilities unfurl against the background of interconnected connections. Grandparents, aunties, uncles, and cousins add to the family's common obligation, offering backing, direction, and a feeling of congruity. Adjusting the requests of present day existence with the significance of keeping up with familial associations turns into an aggregate exertion, building up the interconnectedness that characterizes the nuclear family.

With regards to maturing, the story of adjusting liabilities takes on a piercing shade as families explore the intricacies of eldercare. Generally, the consideration of maturing relatives frequently falls on the shoulders of grown-up kids, mirroring a feeling of obligation established in familial bonds.

The account changes as families embrace cooperative ways to deal with eldercare, recognizing the different qualities and commitments of every part. Adjusting the profound, physical, and calculated parts of eldercare turns into a common obligation, underlining the significance of correspondence, compassion, and shared help.

Mixed families, set apart by the mix of step-guardians, step-kin, and half-kin, face special difficulties in adjusting liabilities and cultivating a feeling of shared obligation. Customarily, cultural assumptions and potential contentions might have presented obstacles inside mixed relational intricacies. The story changes as families focus on open correspondence, adaptability, and a promise to shared liabilities. Adjusting the many-sided trap of connections inside mixed families includes exploring intricacies with grasping, encouraging solidarity, and embracing the common obligation of establishing an amicable family climate.

The account of adjusting liabilities stretches out to the monetary domain, where the cooperative administration of monetary assets becomes fundamental to the family's prosperity. Generally, the job of the provider might have been barely characterized, with an essential spotlight on giving monetary dependability. The story changes as families perceive the different manners by which people can add to the family's monetary wellbeing. Adjusting the obligations of planning, monetary preparation, and navigation includes a common obligation to the family's monetary prosperity.

In the globalized setting, families frequently wrestle with the elements of adjusting work and individual life in a high speed and interconnected world. The account unfurls as people explore the requests of expert obligations while focusing on family time and individual prosperity. Adjusting the quest for vocation objectives with the sustaining of familial associations turns into a common obligation, featuring the significance of adaptability, correspondence, and shared help in accomplishing an amicable balance.

The investigation of obligations interweaves with the idea of close to home work, where the administration of feelings, arrangement of help, and development of good familial associations become indispensable parts of day to day life. Customarily, profound work might have been appointed more to ladies inside the family, reflecting cultural assumptions. The story changes as families perceive the significance of shared profound work, where all individuals effectively add to establishing a sustaining and strong close to home climate. Adjusting the feelings of every relative includes sympathy, undivided attention, and a common obligation to encouraging close to home prosperity.

With regards to familial customs and customs, the story of shared obligation unfurls as relatives meet up to make enduring recollections and build up a feeling of character. Customarily, certain jobs might have been appointed in view old enough or orientation during social functions or familial festivals.

The story changes as families embrace a more comprehensive way to deal with these customs, permitting every part to take an interest and add to the safeguarding of social legacy effectively. Adjusting the obligations of maintaining customs includes an aggregate exertion, supporting the bonds that interface ages and fortify the familial embroidery.

Innovation, while offering exceptional availability, presents new elements that families should explore in their journey to adjust liabilities. The account unfurls as relatives wrestle with the difficulties and potential open doors introduced by innovation, from overseeing screen time to cultivating mindful internet based conduct. Adjusting the advantages of mechanical headways with the requirement for turned off family time turns into a common obligation, mirroring the family's obligation to keeping a sound and associated computerized climate.

Emotional well-being and close to home prosperity are foremost in the investigation of shared obligation inside the family. Customarily, conversations around emotional well-being might have been covered peacefully and disgrace. The story changes as families effectively participate in discussions about psychological wellness, perceiving the significance of shared liabilities in establishing a strong and compassionate climate. Adjusting the feelings of every relative includes an aggregate obligation to focusing on mental prosperity and cultivating open correspondence.

Training, a foundation of day to day life, includes a common obligation to give a steady learning climate to kids. Customarily, guardians might have been viewed as essential teachers, directing youngsters through scholarly pursuits. The story changes as families perceive the common obligations in establishing an all encompassing learning climate that reaches out past proper schooling. Adjusting the requests of scholastic accomplishment with the support of interest and individual development includes an aggregate obligation to encouraging an affection for learning.

The investigation of shared obligation inside the family reaches out to the domain of festivities and achievements, denoting the sections of life. Customarily, certain jobs might have been alloted in light of social or familial assumptions during weddings, birthday celebrations, and other critical occasions. The story changes as families embrace a more customized and comprehensive way to deal with festivities, permitting every part to take an interest and add to the blissful minutes effectively. Adjusting the obligations of arranging and executing festivities includes a common obligation to making enduring recollections and building up the bonds that characterize the nuclear family.

Wellbeing and health, necessary parts of shared obligation, mirror the interconnected idea of familial prosperity. Customarily, certain jobs might have been relegated in view of orientation or mature in issues of medical care and health.

The story changes as families take on a more comprehensive methodology, perceiving the common obligations in advancing wellbeing and prosperity for all individuals. Adjusting the requests of a solid way of life with the consolation of preventive consideration includes an aggregate obligation to supporting each other's prosperity.

Notwithstanding difficulties and emergencies, the story of shared obligation arises as a guide of versatility for the family. Families explore difficulty through an aggregate exertion, drawing on individual qualities and shared liabilities. Adjusting the intricacies of familial emergencies includes cultivating open correspondence, compassion, and a shared obligation to critical thinking. Shared obligation turns into a wellspring of solidarity, empowering families to conquer snags and arise more grounded together.

Dynamic cycles inside the family give a material to the investigation of shared obligation, mirroring the elements of force, authority, and co-operative navigation. Generally, navigation might have been unified, with a patriarch or matron expecting a prevailing job. The story changes as families embrace inclusivity, where every part's voice is esteemed, and obligations are shared. Adjusting the course of direction includes encouraging a feeling of organization, dynamic support, and aggregate liability in controlling the family toward aggregate prosperity.

The investigation of shared obligation inside the family reaches out to the domain of monetary obligations and monetary commitments. Customarily, the job of the provider might have been all the more barely characterized, with an essential spotlight on monetary arrangement. The account changes as families perceive the different manners by which people can add to the family's financial prosperity. Shared liabilities in monetary preparation, planning, and cooperative dynamic become fundamental parts of the account, mirroring the changing scene of familial jobs in financial settings.

The monetary scene of families is many times formed by the assorted gifts, abilities, and yearnings of individual individuals. Adjusting the monetary condition includes a common obligation to open correspondence, laying out monetary objectives, and pursuing informed choices that line up with the family's general prosperity. From overseeing family costs to making arrangements for future undertakings, every relative turns into a functioning member in the monetary account, adding to the common obligation of making monetary security.

With regards to worldwide portability and multicultural encounters, families explore the difficulties and chances of adjusting social variety inside the familial system. The story unfurls as people bring different social foundations, dialects, and customs into the relational peculiarity. Adjusting the mix of various social components includes a common obligation to multifaceted figuring out, liberality, and the festival of variety. Shared obligations reach out to saving social personality, encouraging inclusivity, and exploring the intricacies of multicultural encounters.

The investigation of shared obligation meets with the idea of independence and freedom, especially as youngsters progress into adulthood. Customarily, the shift from reliance to freedom denoted a critical achievement, with grown-up youngsters expecting more independent jobs. In any case, the developing story perceives the significance of reliance, where grown-up youngsters keep up with close associations with their families while seeking after individual objectives and desires. Shared liabilities in supporting each other's processes become necessary to the story of familial bonds that rise above conventional thoughts of autonomy.

Innovation, with its unavoidable impact, presents the two open doors and difficulties in the domain of shared obligation inside the family. The story unfurls as relatives wrestle with the effects of innovation on their day to day routines, connections, and by and large prosperity. Adjusting the advantages of network with the requirement for purposeful turned off time turns into a common obligation, underscoring the significance of adjusting to changing mechanical scenes while saving the quintessence of familial associations. Families effectively participate in discussions about dependable innovation use, computerized decorum, and the cultivating of sound web-based ways of behaving, adding to a common obligation of establishing a reasonable advanced climate.

Psychological wellness and profound prosperity are necessary parts of the account of shared obligation inside the family. Customarily, conversations around emotional well-being might have been covered peacefully and shame. The story changes as families effectively take part in discussions about emotional well-being, perceiving the significance of shared liabilities in establishing a steady and sympathetic climate. Adjusting the feelings of every relative includes an aggregate obligation to focusing on mental prosperity, cultivating open correspondence, and looking for proficient help when required.

With regards to schooling, the story of shared obligation mirrors the significance of encouraging a steady learning climate. Customarily, guardians might have been viewed as essential instructors, directing youngsters through scholarly pursuits. The story changes as families perceive the common obligations in establishing an all encompassing learning climate that stretches out past proper schooling. Kin, grandparents, and more distant family individuals effectively add to the instructive story, offering different viewpoints, enhancing the growth opportunity, and imparting an adoration for deep rooted learning.

The investigation of shared obligation inside the family unfurls with regards to festivities and achievements, denoting the entries of life. Customarily, certain jobs might have been appointed in view of social or familial assumptions during weddings, birthday celebrations, and other huge occasions. The story changes as families embrace a more customized and comprehensive way to deal with festivities, permitting every part to take an interest and add to the euphoric minutes effectively. Adjusting the obligations of arranging and executing festivities includes a common obligation to making enduring recollections and building up the bonds that characterize the nuclear family.

Wellbeing and health, vital parts of shared obligation, mirror the interconnected idea of familial prosperity. Generally, certain jobs might have been allocated in view of orientation or mature in issues of medical services and wellbeing. The story changes as families embrace a more comprehensive methodology, perceiving the common obligations in advancing wellbeing and prosperity for all individuals. Adjusting the requests of a solid way of life with the consolation of preventive consideration includes an aggregate obligation to supporting each other's prosperity.

Even with difficulties and emergencies, the story of shared obligation arises as a reference point of versatility for the family. Families explore difficulty through an aggregate exertion, drawing on individual qualities and shared liabilities. Adjusting the intricacies of familial emergencies includes encouraging open correspondence, sympathy, and a shared obligation to critical thinking. Shared obligation turns into a wellspring of solidarity, empowering families to beat impediments and arise more grounded together.

Dynamic cycles inside the family give a material to the investigation of shared obligation, mirroring the elements of force, authority, and cooperative navigation. Customarily, navigation might have been concentrated, with a patriarch or matron expecting a predominant job. The account changes as families embrace inclusivity, where every part's voice is esteemed, and obligations are shared. Adjusting the course of navigation includes cultivating a feeling of organization, dynamic cooperation, and aggregate liability in controlling the family toward aggregate prosperity.

The sensitive dance of adjusting liabilities and encouraging a feeling of shared obligation inside the family makes an agreeable ensemble of inter-connectedness and common help. From rethinking customary orientation jobs to exploring the intricacies of eldercare, from dealing with the effect of innovation to focusing on emotional well-being, the story mirrors the flexibility, versatility, and cooperative soul that characterize familial con-nections. Adjusting liabilities turns into a craftsmanship, a dance that requires correspondence, compassion, and a common obligation to the prosperity of every relative. As families keep on developing in the always changing scene of cultural assumptions and individual goals, the investi-gation of shared obligation stays a continuous excursion of development, understanding, and the festival of the one of a kind commitments every part brings to the mind boggling movement of familial life.

Chapter 5

"Celebrations of Togetherness"

"Festivities of Fellowship: Sustaining Bonds, Making Recollections, and Embracing Euphoria"

In the embroidered artwork of everyday life, festivities arise as lively strings winding around together snapshots of euphoria, solidarity, and shared encounters. This investigation dives into the complex layers of "Festivities of Harmony," where the ceremonies, customs, and shared minutes become the material whereupon familial bonds are painted. From the conventional to the unprecedented, every festival is a novel section in the family's story, cultivating a feeling of association that rises above time.

At the core of festivities lies the quintessence of association — uniting relatives to check achievements, offer thanks, and revel in the common excursion of life. Generally, festivities have been a demonstration of the aggregate personality of a family, molded by social, strict, and familial customs. Birthday events, commemorations, occasions, and social celebrations become the events where the family merges to make enduring recollections and reinforce the ties that tight spot.

The excellence of festivities lies in the loftiness of the occasion as well as in the effortlessness of shared minutes. Family social events around the supper table, improvised picnics in the patio, or comfortable film evenings at home — this large number of apparently normal events add to the embroidery of harmony. The account of festivities rises above the unprecedented, stressing the worth of regular associations and the delight saw as in the everyday.

Customs and customs structure the foundation of festivities, giving a feeling of progression and shared history to the family story. Whether it's the yearly Thanksgiving feast, the lighting of candles during Diwali, or the trading of presents on Christmas morning, these ceremonies make a feeling of expectation and having a place. Through the progression of time, these customs become the strings that wind around together ages, associating the past, present, and future in an embroidery of familial coherence.

In multicultural and various families, festivities become an investigation of shared personalities and a chance to embrace the wealth of various social foundations. The combination of customs, the mixing of cooking styles, and the fuse of different traditions make a special mosaic that mirrors the family's versatility and receptiveness. Festivities become a scaffold between the old and the new, encouraging multifaceted comprehension and imparting a deep satisfaction in different legacy.

The meaning of festivities stretches out past the substantial — the improvements, the food, and the celebrations. It dwells in the immaterial snapshots of chuckling, shared stories, and the glow of familial associations. These elusive components imbue festivities with a feeling of harmony that rises above the material parts of the occasion. In the giggling shared during a birthday celebration or the tranquil snapshots of reflection during a vacation assembling, the genuine quintessence of festivities is uncovered.

As families explore the intricacies of current life, festivities act as anchors that ground people it could be said of having a place and reason. In the midst of the hurrying around of day to day schedules, festivities offer a delay — a deliberate break to interface, reflect, and offer thanks for the connections that structure the bedrock of day to day life. The purposeful demonstration of meeting up turns into a festival in itself, featuring the significance of cutting out time for shared bliss in the midst of life's requests.

Festivities likewise assume a vital part in molding the profound scene of familial connections. Birthday celebrations, for example, become events to communicate love and appreciation for individual relatives. The demonstration of choosing smart gifts, arranging impromptu get-togethers, and sharing sincere wishes turns into a language of adoration that reinforces the profound bonds inside the family. Also, commemorations become chances to celebrate getting through affection and responsibility, supporting that familial connections are excursions to be appreciated and celebrated.

With regards to familial achievements, festivities become markers of development, change, and shared accomplishments. Graduations, advancements, and other critical life altering situations are honored as individual achievements as well as aggregate triumphs for the family. The demonstration of commending these achievements together cultivates a culture of shared help, where every relative's prosperity is a reason for euphoria for the whole nuclear family.

The account of festivities extends to incorporate the affirmation of difficulties and the flexibility exhibited by relatives during troublesome times. In snapshots of misfortune, meeting up to celebrate little triumphs, show fortitude, and offer thanks for the strength found in aggregate help turns into a strong demonstration of the family's versatility. Festivities become a wellspring of mending, an update that, even despite difficulties, there is space for happiness and fellowship.

As families develop and elements change, the idea of festivities additionally adjusts to mirror the moving scene of familial connections. The introduction of another relative, a wedding, or the inviting of parents in law into the family overlay — this large number of achievements rethink the family story, setting out new open doors for festivities of fellowship. The extension of the nuclear family through relationships and births turns into a festival of individual achievements as well as of the consistent development and reestablishment of the familial embroidery.

The idea of festivities stretches out to the regular thoughtful gestures and appreciation inside the family. The affirmation of little triumphs, the outflow of appreciation for shared liabilities, and the festival of every relative's one of a kind commitments become strings in the texture of day to day existence. The account of festivities embraces the thought that harmony isn't saved for fantastic events alone however is woven into the texture of each and every common second.

In the advanced age, festivities take on new aspects as families explore the difficulties and potential open doors introduced by innovation. Virtual festivals, online social occasions, and the sharing of exceptional minutes through advanced stages become essential parts of the cutting edge family story. The capacity to associate across distances permits families to celebrate harmony in any event, when genuinely separated, featuring the versatile idea of familial securities despite changing mechanical scenes.

The idea of festivities meets with the job of individual relatives in arranging and executing these upbeat events. While specific obligations may generally fall on unambiguous relatives, the developing story of festivities supports a cooperative methodology. Shared obligations in occasion arranging, planning of dinners, and the making of a merry climate become open doors for relatives to add to the delight of the event effectively. This cooperative exertion builds up the possibility that festivals are an aggregate undertaking, where the commitments of every part add to the general feeling of harmony.

The meaning of festivities is additionally emphasizd by the production of family customs that persevere across ages. Whether it's a particular dish served during occasion social events, a yearly family get-away, or an extraordinary approach to trading gifts, these practices become an extension between the past, present, and future. The deliberate reiteration of these ceremonies encourages a feeling of congruity and gives a recognizable structure inside which relatives can make and share new recollections.

As families explore the complexities of different conviction frameworks and strict practices, festivities become a mosaic of otherworldly and social articulations. Strict celebrations, functions, and observances become events for families to meet up in veneration, reflection, and shared commitment. The festival of strict and social customs turns into a hallowed string that ties relatives from a common perspective of direction and otherworldly association.

The quintessence of festivities lies in the making of recollections that persevere past the fleeting delight of the event. The tales shared, the giggling reverberating through the corridors, and the photos catching short lived minutes become engraves on the family's aggregate memory. These recollections, whether safeguarded in a family collection or related during future social occasions, become a gold mine of shared encounters that characterize the novel personality of the family.

5.1 Showcase of joyous family celebrations.

"Exhibit of Upbeat Family Festivities: An Embroidery of Shared Minutes, Love, and Association"

In the kaleidoscope of everyday life, euphoric festivals stand as energetic, vital crossroads that enlighten the common excursion of familial bonds. This investigation digs into the rich embroidery of "Exhibit of Glad Family Festivities," where every occasion turns into a feature of adoration, association, and the winding around together of loved recollections. From the abundance of birthday events to the glow of occasion get-togethers, these festivals are achievements as well as impressions of the persevering through soul of fellowship.

Birthday celebrations, in their substance, epitomize the delight of presence and the enthusiasm for individual individuals inside the family. They act as a yearly marker of development, in age as well as in the lavishness of encounters and the profundity of familial associations. The custom of meeting up to praise a birthday changes the common into the unprecedented, making a space for articulations of affection, appreciation, and shared happiness. Whether set apart by a comfortable family supper, an impromptu get-together, or a basic social event with dear companions, birthday celebrations exhibit the special personality and meaning of every relative.

Commemorations, especially those of guardians or the seniors in the family, become achievements of getting through affection and responsibility. These festivals are an exhibit of the flexibility and strength that structure the groundwork of familial connections.

The demonstration of remembering long stretches of shared encounters, challenges survive, and the persistent excursion of development together turns into a demonstration of the persevering through force of affection inside the family. Whether celebrated with a heartfelt supper, a vacation, or a fabulous social occasion, commemorations feature the excellence of deep rooted organizations and the insight acquired through shared encounters.

Special festivals act as a yearly exhibit of familial practices, social lavishness, and the sorcery of shared celebrations. Whether it's the glow of a Thanksgiving gathering, the delight of Christmas, or the dynamic quality of Diwali, these festivals become features of social personality and the winding around together of customs across ages. The demonstration of meeting up to cook, finish, and take part in social ceremonies turns into a demonstration of the family's flexibility, inclusivity, and the protection of social legacy.

With regards to social and strict celebrations, family festivities become grandstands of otherworldliness, custom, and shared commitment. Celebrations like Eid, Hanukkah, or Lunar New Year become events for families to meet up in worship, petition, and the festival of shared confidence. The exhibit of social and strict celebrations highlights the variety inside the family, encouraging a climate of shared regard, understanding, and the enthusiasm for various conviction frameworks.

Achievement festivities, like graduations and weddings, act as features of individual accomplishments and the interconnectedness of day to day life. Graduations become snapshots of pride and festivity, displaying the perfection of instructive excursions and the aggregate help that moves people toward progress. Weddings, then again, change into great grandstands of adoration, solidarity, and the extension of family ties. The demonstration of praising these achievements together supports that singular accomplishments are shared triumphs for the whole family.

The feature of family festivities reaches out past the stupendous occasions to the domain of regular minutes. Family meals, film evenings, and improvised social affairs become exhibits of shared bliss, giggling, and the excellence tracked down in the effortlessness of harmony. These regular features highlight the possibility that festivals are not bound to explicit dates on the schedule however are woven into the texture of day to day existence, making a persistent embroidery of familial associations.

Customs and customs, woven into the texture of day to day life, become grandstands of coherence, personality, and the progression of time. Whether it's the yearly summer excursion, the practice of baking together during special times of year, or the basic demonstration of sharing stories before sleep time, these ceremonies act as exhibits of shared encounters and the production of enduring recollections. The purposeful reiteration of these customs turns into a feature of the family's obligation to saving a feeling of progression and shared history.

Multigenerational festivities exhibit the interconnectedness of day to day life across various age gatherings. Grandparents, guardians, kids, and grandkids meet up to grandstand the lavishness of assorted viewpoints, encounters, and commitments. These festivals become exhibits of the insight went down through ages, the energy of youth, and the shared discovering that happens inside the nuclear family. The exhibit of multigenerational festivities mirrors the powerful transaction of jobs, obligations, and the repeating idea of familial connections.

In the computerized age, family festivities take on new aspects as innovation fills in as a feature of network across distances. Virtual social occasions, video calls, and the sharing of exceptional minutes through advanced stages become necessary parts of current family exhibits. The capacity to associate across geological limits permits families to feature fellowship in any event, when actually separated, featuring the versatile idea of familial securities notwithstanding changing mechanical scenes.

The demonstration of displaying happy family festivities includes purposeful preparation, cooperation, and the common exertion of all relatives. From choosing subjects for birthday celebrations to organizing surprise occasions, the exhibit of festivities turns into a cooperative undertaking that builds up the significance of shared liabilities. The grandstand of cooperative endeavors highlights that festivals are not the consequence of individual activities but rather are aggregate articulations of affection and fellowship.

In the exhibit of family festivities, the job of individual relatives becomes urgent in arranging, coordinating, and executing occasions. While specific obligations may customarily fall on unambiguous relatives, the developing story of family features empowers a cooperative methodology. Shared obligations in occasion arranging, planning of dinners, and the production of a bubbly air become open doors for relatives to add to the delight of the event effectively. This cooperative exertion builds up the possibility that festivals are an aggregate undertaking, where the commitments of every part add to the general feeling of harmony.

The grandstand of happy family festivities likewise converges with the idea of profound articulation inside familial connections. Festivities give a phase to the exhibit of feelings — articulations of adoration, appreciation, and shared happiness. The demonstration of exhibiting feelings during festivities turns into a language that fortifies the profound bonds inside the family. Whether it's the delight communicated through chuckling, the tears shed during wistful minutes, or the embraces traded in snapshots of festivity, feelings become a necessary piece of the grandstand of familial associations.

Culinary exhibits during family festivities become a tactile encounter that ties relatives together. The demonstration of planning and sharing dinners fills in as a feature of social lavishness, culinary mastery, and the delight tracked down in common eating. Family recipes, went down through ages, become grandstands of culinary customs that characterize the family's personality.

The grandstand of culinary joys during festivities turns into a banquet for the faculties, encouraging a feeling of overflow, and making enduring recollections around the feasting table.

In the exhibit of family festivities, the idea of shared recollections arises as a focal subject. The photos taken, the tales shared, and the encounters made during these festivals become exhibits of shared recollections that persevere past the transient delight of the event. These common recollections act as anchors that interface relatives across time, making a common story that characterizes the exceptional personality of the family. The demonstration of exhibiting recollections turns into an approach to protecting the familial embroidery for people in the future.

Family features reach out to the purposeful development of customs that persevere across ages. Whether it's the yearly family setting up camp excursion, the practice of narrating during occasion social events, or the one of a kind way certain festivals are denoted, these customs become grandstands of progression, character, and the progression of time. The purposeful reiteration of these customs turns into an exhibit of the family's obligation to protecting a feeling of congruity and shared history.

5.2 Shared memories of special occasions.

"Shared Recollections of Unique Events: Supporting the Heartbeat of Familial Bonds"

In the embroidery of everyday life, the strings of shared recollections woven through extraordinary events make an energetic and persevering through mosaic. This investigation digs into the embodiment of "Shared Recollections of Exceptional Events," where every festival turns into a part in the aggregate story of familial bonds. From the euphoric reverberation of chuckling during occasions to the powerful minutes carved in the texture of achievements, these common recollections embody the heartbeat of everyday life, producing associations that rise above time.

Occasions stand as piercing materials for the production of shared recollections, painting day to day existence with strokes of fellowship, bliss, and custom. Whether it's the bubbly environment of Christmas, the intelligent soul of Thanksgiving, or the celebratory energy of New Year's Eve, occasions become embroideries of shared encounters. The common recollections of enlivening the Christmas tree, setting up a Thanksgiving gala, or counting down to the 12 PM hour on New Year's Eve engrave permanent engravings on the aggregate memory of the family.

Birthday celebrations, as individual achievements, arise as parts in the common memory book of day to day life. The yearly festival of every relative's introduction to the world turns into a material for articulations of affection, appreciation, and the production of enduring recollections. The common memory of impromptu get-togethers, genuine presents, and the aggregate singing of "Blissful Birthday" turns into a custom that draws upbeat engravings on the hearts of both the celebrant and the whole family.

Weddings, as a festival of association and congruity, hold a unique spot in the display of shared recollections. The common memory of strolling down the path, trading promises, and seeing the solidarity of two families turns into a piercing part in the family's aggregate story. Wedding services, with their customs and customs, become shared recollections that tight spot the couple as well as weave associations among more distant family individuals, making an embroidery of affection and solidarity.

Commemorations, whether stamping long periods of marriage or other huge achievements, become shared recollections that celebrate persevering through affection and responsibility. The common memory of commemoration festivities, whether through cozy meals or great social events, turns into a demonstration of the strength of familial bonds and the affirmation of shared ventures. These common recollections act as anchors, helping relatives to remember the magnificence tracked down in responsibility, support, and the progression of time.

Family excursions, with their kaleidoscope of encounters, become lively sections in the common memory book. The common memory of investigating new spots, setting out on experiences, and exploring the complexities of movement turns into an embroidery of holding and revelation. Whether it's the chuckling shared on an ocean side get-away or the stunningness motivated minutes during a social campaign, family excursions make shared recollections that persevere as previews of happiness and harmony.

Social and strict festivals become exhibits of shared customs, ceremonies, and the protection of legacy. The common memory of lighting candles during Diwali, breaking diets together during Ramadan, or partaking in social functions turns into a declaration to the variety inside the family. These common recollections celebrate social wealth as well as act as scaffolds that interface ages, cultivating an appreciation for the qualities implanted in social and strict practices.

The common memory of familial achievements, like graduations, advancements, and accomplishments, turns into a wellspring of aggregate pride and festivity. The common memory of cheering achievements, partaking in the fervor of fresh starts, and offering support during moves turns into a demonstration of the interconnectedness of day to day life. Achievement minutes act as anchors in the common memory bank, mirroring the aggregate interest in every relative's excursion.

In the domain of regular day to day existence, apparently conventional minutes become shared recollections that characterize the surface of familial connections. The common memory of family meals, film evenings, and unconstrained trips turns into an exhibition of regular bliss. These common recollections, woven into the texture of day to day existence, grandstand the excellence tracked down in effortlessness, making a constant story of fellowship that rises above the exceptional.

Customs and customs, as the strings restricting everyday life, become features of shared recollections that span ages. The common memory of yearly customs, whether it's the cutting of a Thanksgiving turkey, the lighting of candles on a birthday cake, or the perusing of a loved sleep time story, turns into a hallowed engraving in the family's shared mindset. These common recollections act as standards, establishing relatives it could be said of coherence and shared history.

Multigenerational social events become exhibits of shared recollections that feature the interconnectedness of everyday life across various age gatherings. The common memory of grandparents sharing stories, youngsters playing with cousins, and guardians organizing the agreeable tumult of family social occasions turns into a display of generational associations. These common recollections, frequently established in the wistfulness of past get-togethers, make a feeling of having a place and coherence for every relative.

In the computerized age, innovation fills in as both a material and a vehicle for the making of shared recollections. Virtual festivals, video calls, and the sharing of unique minutes through computerized stages become necessary parts of present day family memory-production. The common memory of virtual family gatherings, online birthday festivities, and the trading of computerized photograph collections turns into a demonstration of the flexibility of familial bonds even with changing innovative scenes.

Culinary encounters, in their tangible extravagance, become shared recollections that tight spot relatives together. The common memory of cooking together, sharing feasts, and relishing conventional dishes turns into a gastronomic excursion that reflects the lavishness of familial associations. Family recipes, went down through ages, become shared recollections that tempt taste buds as well as act as unmistakable connections to social legacy and familial character.

In the exhibit of shared recollections, the demonstration of narrating turns into a strong vehicle for the transmission of family legend. The common memory of describing tales, remembering previous encounters, and passing down familial stories turns into a custom that reinforces the familial embroidery. These common recollections, frequently decorated with chuckling, tears, and the subtleties of oral practice, become the account string that interfaces relatives across time.

The demonstration of gift-giving, whether during occasions or extraordinary events, turns into an unmistakable portrayal of shared recollections. The common memory of choosing insightful gifts, wrapping them with care, and seeing the delight on a friend or family member's face turns into a language of adoration inside the family. These common recollections of gift trades not just mirror the care of individual relatives yet in addition act as badge of warmth that persevere past the snapshot of opening up.

The idea of shared recollections converges with the outflow of feelings inside familial connections. The common memory of chuckling during festivities, the tears shed during impactful minutes, and the embraces traded in the midst of satisfaction or distress become profound engravings on the aggregate heart of the family. Feelings, woven into the texture of shared recollections, make a reverberation that extends the bonds among relatives.

The common memory of defeating difficulties and exploring emergencies turns into a demonstration of the flexibility of familial bonds. Whether it's enduring monetary difficulties, supporting each other through wellbeing emergencies, or confronting outside misfortunes, the common memory of aggregate strength turns into a wellspring of motivation and backbone. These common recollections of beating difficulties act as updates that familial bonds are produced in snapshots of satisfaction as well as in the cauldron of shared misfortune.

Family get-togethers, whether arranged or unconstrained, become exhibits of shared recollections that rise above topographical distances. The common memory of reconnecting with family members, sharing stories, and making new recollections together turns into a festival of genealogy and the interconnectedness of more distant family life. These common recollections of reunions act as anchors that tie relatives to their foundations, encouraging a feeling of having a place and congruity.

In the feature of shared recollections, the idea of deliberate memory-production arises as a cognizant work to make and safeguard significant minutes. The common memory of arranging impromptu get-togethers, coordinating family relaxes, or starting new practices turns into an impression of the family's obligation to winding around an embroidery of harmony. Purposeful memory-production highlights that common recollections are not exclusively the result of luck but rather additionally the consequence of conscious activities that focus on familial associations.

Inside the feature of shared recollections, the idea of family customs arises as a radiant string, it its way through the aggregate story to wind around. These practices become grandstands of congruity, personality, and the progression of time. The common memory of repeating ceremonies, whether it's the yearly family setting up camp outing, the custom of Sunday early lunch, or the special way certain festivals are stamped, turns into a grandstand of purposeful memory-production.

Family customs, by their actual nature, are exhibits of shared recollections that span ages. The common memory of passing down recipes starting with one age then onto the next, educating grandkids the craft of narrating, or taking part in age-old family customs turns into a living declaration to the interconnectedness of everyday life across various age gatherings. These common recollections inside the setting of family customs make a feeling of heritage, permitting every age to add to and acquire the rich embroidery of familial encounters.

In the domain of family customs, festivities take on an exceptional importance. The common memory of explicit customs related with birthday celebrations, occasions, and other extraordinary events turns into a feature of purposeful memory-production. Whether it's how birthday events are commended with an extraordinary family custom or the particular way occasions are set apart with explicit traditions, these common recollections mirror the family's obligation to making a feeling of character and coherence.

The common memory of family get-togethers, as a necessary piece of familial practices, turns into a celebratory exhibit that rises above time and distance. The common memory of social occasion with family members, restoring associations, and taking part in shared exercises turns into a living material of familial bonds. These common recollections inside the setting of family gatherings act as standards, establishing relatives it could be said of having a place, cultivating solidarity, and making a residing demonstration of the perseverance of family ties.

The demonstration of making family customs and purposeful memory-production stretches out to the festival of social legacy. The common memory of partaking in social celebrations, noticing customs went down through ages, and participating in exercises that reflect social character turns into an exhibit of variety inside the family. These common recollections become festivities of social lavishness, encouraging a climate of inclusivity, regard, and appreciation for the uniqueness that every relative brings to the aggregate embroidered artwork.

In the feature of shared recollections, the idea of heritage building becomes entwined with the purposeful production of family customs. The common memory of more established ages conferring insight, sharing life illustrations, and setting out open doors for more youthful relatives to interface with their foundations turns into a demonstration of the passing down of a familial heritage. These common recollections inside the setting of heritage building act as signals, directing relatives in exploring their singular processes while residual established in the qualities and customs that characterize the family's personality.

Family customs, as features of shared recollections, cross with the idea of flexibility inside familial connections. The common memory of taking part in customs during testing times, tracking down comfort in natural ceremonies, and drawing strength from the congruity of family customs turns into a strong grandstand of aggregate flexibility. These common recollections inside the setting of family customs act as anchors, offering dependability and a feeling of business as usual even notwithstanding difficulty.

In the computerized age, the formation of shared recollections and family customs takes on new aspects as innovation turns into an exhibit of network. The common memory of making computerized photograph collections, recording extraordinary minutes through recordings, and partaking in virtual family customs turns into a versatile reaction to changing mechanical scenes. These common recollections, worked with by innovation, act as a contemporary exhibit of familial bonds that rise above actual distances.

The feature of shared recollections inside family customs accentuates the purposeful development of happy minutes, even amidst regular schedules. The common memory of implanting normal exercises with a feeling of festivity — whether it's how breakfast is served on a Sunday morning or the practice of sharing everyday features during supper — turns into an exhibit of tracking down delight in the straightforwardness of fellowship. These common recollections highlight the possibility that each second, regardless of how unremarkable, can be changed into a significant festival inside the familial setting.

Inside the feature of shared recollections, the demonstration of returning to past customs and ceremonies turns into a type of time travel — an approach to reconnect with the quintessence of familial bonds. The common memory of reviving an old family custom, returning to a valued action from an earlier time, or reviving the fire of a once-darling custom turns into a feature of coherence and the recurrent idea of everyday life. These common recollections inside the setting of returning to customs act as a wellspring of sentimentality and a festival of the persevering through nature of familial associations.

Family customs, as grandstands of shared recollections, converge with the idea of appreciation inside familial connections. The common memory of offering thanks during explicit customs, recognizing the meaning of shared minutes, and setting out open doors for reflection turns into a feature of appreciation for the endowments inside the family. These common recollections inside the setting of offering thanks act as a wake up call of the significance of recognizing and praising the wealth of adoration, support, and shared encounters inside the familial structure.

The grandstand of shared recollections inside family customs shapes a glowing embroidery that catches the essence of familial bonds. Whether through the purposeful making of ceremonies, the festival of social legacy, or the passing down of inheritance, family customs become exhibits of progression, character, and the persevering through nature of familial associations. These common recollections inside the setting of family customs act as a demonstration of the lavishness of familial life, praising the delight found in purposeful memory-production and the immortal reverberation of fellowship.

5.3 Illustration of how collective joy is amplified during festivities.

"Delineation of Aggregate Happiness: Enhancing Fellowship during Celebrations"

In the many-sided dance of everyday life, celebrations arise as ensembles of aggregate happiness, where individual notes orchestrate to make a song that reverberates through the hallways of familial securities. This investigation digs into the embroidery of "Aggregate Delight during Merriments," showing how the festival of unique events changes into a common encounter that intensifies harmony, fortifies associations, and leaves a permanent engraving on the aggregate memory of the family.

Merriments, whether established in social practices, strict observances, or individual achievements, become exhibits of aggregate bliss that unite relatives from a sense of festivity. The common experience of getting ready for merriments turns into a preface to the happy crescendo, meshing fervor and expectation into the actual texture of day to day life. The cooperative exertion of brightening spaces, arranging feasts, and taking part in bubbly customs turns into a grandstand of aggregate contribution that enhances the feeling of harmony.

With regards to social and strict merriments, the common memory of taking part in ceremonies turns into a distinctive outline of aggregate delight. Whether it's the lighting of candles during Diwali, the breaking of diets together during Ramadan, or the trading of presents on Christmas morning, these ceremonies act as central focuses that enhance the common experience of euphoria inside the family. The reverberation of aggregate supplications, serenades, or stately practices turns into a strong representation of how celebrations act as channels for shared profound encounters.

The common memory of getting ready happy dinners turns into a tactile festival that enhances aggregate satisfaction through taste, smell, and public feasting. The demonstration of cooking together, sharing family recipes, and enjoying bubbly dining experiences turns into an exhibit of culinary cooperation. Bubbly feasts act as a dinner of shared encounters, delineating how the demonstration of eating together enhances the flavors on the table as well as the bonds that tie relatives in a common embroidery of bliss.

Enrichments, whether decorating the home or checking happy spaces, become visual outlines of aggregate delight during celebrations. The common memory of decking the corridors, hanging lights, or making complex rangoli plans turns into a demonstration of the aggregate exertion put resources into intensifying the happy air. The visual display of bubbly beautifications changes actual spaces as well as fills in as a visual sign of the delight imbued into each edge of the family's common climate.

Gift-giving, a fundamental piece of numerous merriments, turns into an impactful representation of aggregate bliss as relatives trade badge of affection and friendship. The common memory of choosing smart gifts, wrapping them with care, and seeing the delight on the essences of friends and family during the trade turns into a grandstand of close to home reverberation. The demonstration of giving and getting gifts enhances the delight inside familial connections, showing how these motions become unmistakable articulations of affection that add to the aggregate festival.

In the domain of familial achievements and individual accomplishments, festivities become representations of aggregate bliss that enhance the feeling of achievement. Whether it's a graduation, an advancement, or a critical individual accomplishment, the common memory of supporting the individual turns into a clear outline of aggregate unrivaled delight.

These celebratory minutes feature individual achievements as well as act as any open doors for the family to intensify the delight felt by every part, building up the possibility that triumphs are shared and celebrated by and large.

The common memory of happy clothing turns into a visual delineation of how aggregate delight is enhanced through the demonstration of sprucing up for exceptional events. Whether it's wearing customary pieces of clothing, planning outfits, or embracing a merry clothing standard, the common experience of picking clothing turns into a feature of solidarity and shared excitement. Merry dress turns into a type of visual narrating, delineating how individual articulations of style merge to make an aggregate stylish that intensifies the by and large euphoric climate.

Music and dance, essential parts of numerous merriments, become hear-able outlines of aggregate euphoria that reverberate through the air. The common memory of singing together, moving to bubbly tunes, or playing instruments turns into an ensemble of harmony. The aggregate articulation of satisfaction through music and dance enhances the happy soul, making an environment where individual articulations of delight consistently mix into an amicable festival that rises above individual limits.

Family customs, woven into the texture of celebrations, become living delineations of how aggregate delight is enhanced across ages. The common memory of passing down customs, taking part in exercises that have been essential for the family for quite a long time, and seeing the energy of more youthful relatives turns into a grandstand of coherence and association. Bubbly customs become spans that range ages, enhancing the delight experienced by every part as they add to and acquire the aggregate festival.

With regards to multigenerational social affairs, the common memory of seniors conferring astuteness, sharing stories, and taking part in happy exercises turns into a delineation of how aggregate satisfaction is improved through the insight of involvement. The interaction of points of view, energy, and commitments across various age bunches makes a lively representation of familial bonds that enhance satisfaction during merriments. The giggling of kids, the insight of elderly folks, and the energy of in the middle between meet to make a multi-generational festival that rises above individual encounters.

The common memory of establishing happy conditions stretches out past the actual domain to the computerized scene, delineating how innovation turns into an instrument for enhancing aggregate satisfaction. Virtual festivals, video calls, and the sharing of happy minutes through computerized stages become outlines of how innovation spans separates and associates relatives in the festival. The virtual space turns into a material where aggregate delight is shared, intensified, and experienced together, in any event, when actual distances present difficulties.

Merriments, as representations of aggregate delight, converge with the idea of deliberate memory-production inside familial connections. The common memory of arranging and executing bubbly festivals purposefully turns into an outline of the family's obligation to making enduring impressions. The purposeful mixture of happiness into merriments highlights that aggregate festivals are not simple chance occurrences but rather intentional demonstrations that add to the continuous account of familial fellowship.

Amidst aggregate bliss during celebrations, the demonstration of offering thanks turns into an impactful outline of appreciation and association. The common memory of communicating gratitude for the presence of friends and family, recognizing the endeavors put resources into making a happy climate, and considering the favors inside the family turns into an intensification of appreciation. Merriments become events for happiness as well as for the purposeful acknowledgment of the overflow tracked down in familial connections.

The common memory of beating difficulties and exploring expected clashes during celebrations turns into a representation of the flexibility inside familial bonds. The demonstration of meeting up, figuring out some shared interest, and by and large making an air of satisfaction even with potential snags turns into a strong representation of familial solidarity. Merriments act as any open doors to grandstand the strength of aggregate bonds and the capacity to beat difficulties through shared delight.

With regards to social and cultural variety, merriments become delineations of consideration and acknowledgment inside the family. The common memory of embracing and celebrating different social practices, strict observances, or individual inclinations intensifies the feeling of solidarity inside the familial woven artwork. Merriments become stages for recognizing and valuing the variety that every relative brings, making a comprehensive air where euphoria is amplified through shared regard and understanding.

Inside the grandstand of aggregate bliss during merriments, the idea of shared liabilities arises as a necessary part of the festival. The common memory of teaming up on different assignments — whether it's cooking, brightening, or arranging exercises — turns into a delineation of how obligations are dispersed to enhance the generally merry experience. Shared liabilities become strings that wind around together the aggregate delight of the family, supporting that the festival is a cooperative exertion where each part assumes a crucial part.

Inside the charming domain of aggregate satisfaction during merriments, the demonstration of narrating turns into a story outline that winds around together the strings of familial associations. The common memory of recapping stories, remembering previous encounters, and sharing tales during happy social affairs turns into a sly articulation of aggregate bliss. Narrating turns into a medium through which the family considers its common history, making a nonstop story that enhances the happy climate of the festival.

The common memory of narrating during celebrations fills in as a scaffold between ages, an outline of how the insight of elderly folks and the excitement of more youthful relatives join to make a rich embroidery of aggregate delight. Whether it's the retelling of appreciated family stories, describing the historical backdrop of explicit customs, or sharing individual encounters connected with the merriments, narrating turns into an intuitive delineation that improves the familial festival.

The craft of narrating during celebrations reaches out to the purposeful development of family legend, turning into a living delineation of the family's remarkable personality and shared history. The common memory of passing down stories starting with one age then onto the next turns into a deliberate demonstration of protecting the familial story. Celebrations act as events where these accounts show some major signs of life, enhancing the delight of shared encounters and making a feeling of coherence that ranges across time.

With regards to social and strict merriments, narrating turns into a representation of legacy conservation and the festival of aggregate personality. The common memory of describing social fantasies, strict stories, or authentic stories turns into a purposeful demonstration of communicating values, convictions, and social extravagance. Narrating during celebrations turns into a lively representation of how aggregate delight is entwined with a profound appreciation for the social and strict embroidery that characterizes the family.

The common memory of making and describing one of a kind family customs turns into a type of narrating that intensifies the glad air during celebrations. Whether it's the history of a specific practice, the development of bubbly ceremonies, or the funny tales related with explicit traditions, narrating turns into a deliberate demonstration that implants the festival with chuckling, meaning, and a common feeling of association.

Inside the embroidery of narrating during celebrations, the common memory of making new accounts turns into an outline of versatility and the developing idea of familial bonds. Celebrations give valuable open doors to the family to make new stories, share late encounters, and make new recollections that add to the continuous story. The deliberate demonstration of narrating turns into a festival of the present, delineating how the family's aggregate happiness stretches out past the limits of custom to embrace the steadily changing elements of familial connections.

The common memory of humor and giggling implanted into narrating during merriments turns into a delineation of the carefree soul that intensifies delight inside the family. Whether it's the retelling of entertaining stories, the lively relating of past capers, or the production of bubbly jokes, humor turns into an energetic string in the familial story. The common chuckling turns into a hear-able delineation of bliss, reverberating through the bubbly space and making a climate of cheer.

With regards to familial achievements and individual accomplishments commended during merriments, narrating turns into a representation of shared unparalleled delight. The common memory of describing the excursion prompting an accomplishment, sharing the difficulties survive, and communicating aggregate pride turns into a story representation that enhances the celebratory soul. Narrating turns into a vehicle through which relatives commend each other's triumphs, making an aggregate story of progress and satisfaction.

The common memory of making fictitious stories or inventive accounts during merriments turns into an outline of the imaginative soul that intensifies satisfaction inside the family. Whether it's the creating of a bubbly themed story, the development of fantastical characters, or the investigation of innovative domains, narrating turns into a perky representation that rises above the real world. The demonstration of inventive narrating turns into a common undertaking that adds a layer of eccentricity and happiness to the familial festival.

Inside the computerized age, narrating during merriments takes on new aspects as innovation turns into an instrument for sharing and protecting stories. The common memory of making computerized photograph collections, recording video messages, or arranging on the web stages for family stories turns into a delineation of how innovation enhances the compass and effect of familial accounts. The computerized space turns into a virtual material where narrating turns into an intelligent and dynamic delineation of aggregate delight.

The common memory of reporting and documenting family stories during celebrations turns into a purposeful representation of heritage building. Whether through the production of a family diary, the gathering of video files, or the improvement of a computerized storehouse, narrating turns into a purposeful demonstration that adds to the conservation of the family's aggregate memory. Celebrations act as events where these accounts are returned to, shared, and developed, intensifying the feeling of association and coherence.

Amidst narrating during celebrations, the idea of shared feelings arises as a necessary representation inside familial connections. The common memory of communicating feelings — whether through bittersweet tears euphoria, snapshots of sincere appreciation, or the common warmth of giggling — turns into a close to home representation that enhances the familial festival. Narrating turns into a medium through which relatives express their most profound sentiments, making a close to home reverberation that upgrades the general feeling of delight.

The common memory of narrating during celebrations crosses with the idea of inclusivity and the affirmation of assorted viewpoints inside the family. Celebrations become events where different relatives are welcome to share their accounts, offer their one of a kind points of view, and add to the general story. Narrating turns into a comprehensive outline that praises the variety inside the family, cultivating a climate where each voice is esteemed and each story is woven into the aggregate embroidery of satisfaction.

Inside the woven artwork of narrating during celebrations, the demonstration of reflection turns into a deliberate outline of appreciation and appreciation. The common memory of pondering the meaning of family stories, offering thanks for shared encounters, and recognizing the interconnectedness of familial bonds turns into an intelligent representation that enhances the cheerful environment. Narrating turns into a medium through which relatives respite to see the value in the wealth of their aggregate story and the delight tracked down in shared minutes.

The common memory of defeating difficulties and exploring likely struggles through narrating during celebrations turns into a delineation of versatility inside familial connections. The demonstration of sharing accounts of versatility, relating snapshots of solidarity notwithstanding difficulty, and on the whole recognizing difficulties turns into a story representation that enhances the familial festival. Narrating turns into a vehicle through which relatives certify their capacity to beat impediments together, making a story of shared strength and delight.

The outline of narrating during merriments reveals a unique story that improves the familial festival with profundity, feeling, and network. Whether through the retelling of appreciated family stories, the making of creative accounts, or the deliberate documentation of family legend, narrating turns into a sly articulation that enhances the cheerful air. Merriments act as events where narrating turns into a public undertaking, making a common story that rises above individual encounters and adds to the getting through embroidery of familial bonds. The aggregate happiness experienced during merriments becomes a festival of the current second as well as a purposeful delineation of the family's continuous story — a story woven with strings of stories that tight spot, interface, and reverberate through the reverberations of shared delight.

Chapter 6

"Crisis and Compassion"

In the mind boggling embroidery of day to day life, the strings of emergency and sympathy meet to make a significant story of versatility, compassion, and interconnectedness. This investigation dives into the complicated territory of "Emergency and Empathy" inside familial connections, delineating how snapshots of difficulty become pots for the sign of aggregate strength, support, and immovable love.

Emergency, as an inescapable feature of life, creates its shaded area across the familial scene, introducing difficulties that can go from individual battles to outer afflictions. The common memory of exploring these emergencies turns into an indispensable piece of the family's aggregate story — a story that unfurls with snapshots of difficulty, weakness, and the crude real factors of the human experience. Notwithstanding emergency, the nuclear family turns into a safe-haven where the complexities of empathy, understanding, and common help are enlightened.

The common memory of confronting wellbeing emergencies inside the family fills in as a piercing delineation of how sympathy turns into a directing power in the midst of weakness.

Whether it's a significant sickness, a health related crisis, or the drawn out difficulties of a constant condition, the aggregate reaction of the family turns into a strong delineation of unqualified love. The common memory of going with a relative to clinical arrangements, offering daily reassurance during medicines, and exploring the intricacies of medical services turns into a demonstration of the sympathy that twists inside familial connections during snapshots of wellbeing emergencies.

Monetary difficulties, as a type of emergency, become a common encounter that enlightens the interconnectedness of day to day life. The common memory of exploring monetary difficulties, enduring monetary

119

vulnerabilities, and altogether finding answers for financial difficulties turns into an outline of flexibility and empathy. The nuclear family turns into an organization of help where individuals contribute, adjust, and co-operate to explore the tempest of monetary emergency, encouraging a feeling of shared liability and common comprehension.

The common memory of exploring pain and misfortune turns into a significant representation of sympathy as the family revitalizes together to give comfort and backing. Whether grieving the departure of a friend or family member, confronting the difficulties of deprivation, or by and large regarding the memory of the individuals who have passed, the family turns into a safe-haven of empathy where the subtleties of distress are recognized and shared. The common memory of holding each other through tears, thinking back about valued minutes, and finding strength in aggregate grieving turns into a demonstration of the persevering through nature of familial empathy.

With regards to individual emergencies, for example, character battles, emotional well-being difficulties, or existential addressing, the family's reaction turns into a delineation of sympathy as a mending force. The common memory of tuning in without judgment, offering genuine help, and by and large looking for assets for individual prosperity turns into a story of familial sympathy. Sympathy turns into an extension that inter-faces relatives in their singular processes, making a space where weak-nesses are embraced, and the intricacies of individual emergencies are explored by and large.

Catastrophic events, outer emergencies, or unanticipated occasions that disturb the family's harmony become shared encounters that high-light the significance of sympathy in the midst of vulnerability. The common memory of on the whole enduring tempests, supporting each other through unexpected difficulties, and modifying together turns into a representation of familial strength notwithstanding outside emergen-cies. The nuclear family turns into a shelter where sympathy isn't simply stretched out to its individuals yet in addition transmits outward, making a gradually expanding influence of compassion that reaches out to the more extensive local area.

The common memory of confronting social emergencies inside the family — like struggles, false impressions, or strains — turns into a repre-sentation of empathy as a mending demulcent.

The aggregate endeavors to explore clashes, participate in open cor-respondence, and cultivate grasping become a demonstration of the strength of familial bonds. Sympathy turns into an extraordinary power that permits relatives to rise above contrasts, figure out something worth agreeing on, and revamp trust in the fallout of social emergencies.

Empathy, as a continuous account inside familial connections, meets with the idea of pardoning. The common memory of broadening pardoning, looking for compromise, and on the whole pushing ahead from snapshots of harmed or double-crossing turns into an outline of sympathy as an impetus for recuperating. The family turns into a cauldron where pardoning isn't just conceded yet in addition effectively developed, making a space where sympathy turns into a core value during the time spent remaking and fortifying familial bonds.

With regards to outer difficulties, like cultural emergencies, political disturbances, or social moves, the family turns into a microcosm where sympathy fills in as a balancing out force. The common memory of aggregately handling outside emergencies, taking part in significant conversations, and exploring the effect of bigger cultural powers turns into an outline of familial versatility. Sympathy turns into a scaffold that interfaces relatives to the more extensive world, encouraging a comprehension of shared mankind and a pledge to exploring outside difficulties with compassion and solidarity.

The common memory of confronting instructive difficulties, profession mishaps, or individual dissatisfactions inside the family turns into an outline of sympathy as a wellspring of consolation and backing. Whether it's exploring scholarly battles, adapting to employment misfortune, or conquering mishaps, the family turns into a harbor where sympathy pushes people forward. The common memory of offering support, giving a security net during snapshots of vulnerability, and all in all celebrating little triumphs turns into a demonstration of the sympathetic establishment that underlies familial connections.

In the computerized age, innovation becomes both a vehicle for correspondence during emergencies and a delineation of the versatility of familial empathy. The common memory of virtual help, video calls during troublesome times, and the utilization of computerized stages to remain associated turns into a representation of how innovation works with the augmentation of empathy across geological distances. The family turns into an organization where the force of virtual association improves the aggregate reaction to emergencies, guaranteeing that sympathy rises above actual limits.

Inside the familial story of emergency and sympathy, the demonstration of purposeful correspondence turns into a urgent delineation of compassion and understanding. The common memory of family gatherings, open exchanges, and purposeful conversations during emergencies turns into a representation of how empathy flourishes in a climate of straightforward correspondence.

The family turns into a space where people feel appreciated, comprehended, and upheld, encouraging a culture of empathy that saturates each feature of the familial excursion.

The common memory of working together on critical thinking during emergencies turns into an outline of aggregate strength and empathy. Whether it's conceptualizing arrangements, looking for proficient guidance, or preparing assets, the family turns into a group that explores difficulties together. Empathy turns into the main thrust that moves cooperative endeavors, guaranteeing that the aggregate strength of the family is tackled to beat emergencies and arise more grounded.

The idea of shared liabilities inside the family turns into a vital outline of sympathy during seasons of emergency. The common memory of conveying errands, on the whole overseeing liabilities, and effectively taking part in the goal of difficulties turns into a story of familial help. Sympathy turns into an unmistakable power that guides relatives in bearing the weights of emergency together, supporting that the aggregate strength of the family is more noteworthy than the amount of its singular parts.

The common memory of cultivating a feeling of predictability during emergencies turns into a delineation of sympathy as a settling force. Whether it's keeping up with schedules, making snapshots of satisfaction in the midst of difficulties, or purposefully sustaining a positive climate, the family turns into a safe-haven where sympathy turns into an encouraging sign. Empathy turns into a core value that helps relatives to remember the flexibility tracked down in shared snapshots of predictability, even amidst emergency.

In the repercussions of emergencies, the common memory of aggregate reflection turns into a delineation of the groundbreaking force of empathy. Whether it's recognizing the illustrations picked up, commending achievements of recuperation, or on the whole offering thanks for the help got, the family turns into a material where sympathy paints a story of development and strength. Sympathy turns into a compass that guides relatives toward a common future set apart by strength, understanding, and an extended appreciation for the bonds that endure the trial of emergency.

The investigation of "Emergency and Sympathy" inside familial connections divulges a story that unpredictably winds around together the intricacies of misfortune and the groundbreaking influence of compassion. From wellbeing emergencies and monetary difficulties to social contentions and outside disturbances, the family arises as a pot where sympathy turns into the directing power that changes snapshots of emergency into valuable open doors for aggregate development. The common memory of exploring emergencies and stretching out empathy turns into a demonstration of the getting through nature of familial bonds — a story that, even notwithstanding difficulty, enlightens the flexibility, strength, and unflinching affection that characterizes the familial excursion.

6.1 Examination of how the family handles crises.

In the complex embroidery of day to day life, the assessment of how the family handles emergencies turns into a significant investigation of flexibility, versatility, and the interconnectedness of familial bonds. This excursion dives into the complex elements of emergency reaction inside the nuclear family, revealing insight into the components, methodologies, and shared accounts that arise despite difficulty.

The common memory of how the family handles wellbeing emergencies turns into a piercing point of convergence in understanding the strength implanted inside familial connections. Whether wrestling with a difficult sickness, a health related crisis, or the intricacies of overseeing persistent circumstances, the family turns into a safe-haven where sympathy, compassion, and aggregate strength unite. The assessment of how the family explores wellbeing emergencies uncovers a story of unfaltering help, from going with friends and family to clinical arrangements to effectively partaking in providing care liabilities.

Monetary difficulties, as a type of emergency, become a focal point through which the family's reaction mirrors its versatile limits. The assessment of how the family handles monetary emergencies uncovers an embroidery woven with joint effort, vital preparation, and a common obligation to enduring the hardship together. The nuclear family changes into an aggregate asset, where individuals contribute their assets, pool assets, and explore the complexities of financial difficulties with strength and a feeling of shared liability.

The common memory of how the family handles pain and misfortune gives experiences into the capacity to appreciate anyone on a deeper level and emotionally supportive networks that support familial connections. When confronted with the significant difficulties of loss, the family turns into a safe-haven of sympathy, offering comfort, understanding, and an aggregate space for grieving. The assessment of how the family explores sadness uncovers a story of shared recognition, recognizing the effect of misfortune, and cultivating a climate where the intricacies of grieving are met with compassion and public strength.

In the domain of individual emergencies, for example, character battles, psychological wellness challenges, or existential addressing, the family's reaction turns into a demonstration of its flexibility and obligation to individual prosperity. The assessment of how the family handles individual emergencies highlights the significance of open correspondence, destigmatization of psychological well-being, and an aggregate obligation to supporting every part's excursion. The family develops into a place of refuge where weaknesses are embraced, encouraging a story of compassion, understanding, and a common obligation to individual development.

Outer emergencies, going from catastrophic events to cultural disturbances, become shared encounters that feature the family's job as a microcosm inside the bigger setting. The assessment of how the family handles outside emergencies uncovers a story of aggregate flexibility, versatility, and a guarantee to local area. Whether confronting the effect of cataclysmic events or exploring the intricacies of cultural difficulties, the family turns into a unit that expands its empathy past its limits, delineating the interconnectedness between familial bonds and the more extensive world.

The common memory of how the family handles social emergencies — clashes, mistaken assumptions, or strains — offers bits of knowledge into the groundworks of correspondence, pardoning, and the limit with respect to development inside familial connections. The assessment of how the family explores social emergencies uncovers a story of undivided attention, helpful discourse, and a promise to recuperating. The family turns into a powerful space where clashes are met with sympathy, cultivating a climate where social flexibility and grasping become indispensable to the familial story.

Sympathy, as a common topic inside emergency reaction, crosses with the idea of pardoning. The assessment of how the family handles emergencies from the perspective of pardoning uncovers a story of beauty, lowliness, and the limit with respect to development. Whether exploring clashes, beating difficulties, or tending to individual deficiencies, the family turns into a pot where pardoning turns into a groundbreaking power, adding to the continuous story of familial bonds fortified through empathy.

With regards to instructive difficulties, vocation mishaps, or individual disillusionments, the family's reaction turns into a delineation of its job as an encouraging group of people. The assessment of how the family handles emergencies connected with training or vocation discloses a story of consolation, strength, and a guarantee to aggregate headway. The family turns into a center where misfortunes are met with sympathy, and where the common memory of exploring moves turns into a demonstration of the persevering through help woven into the texture of familial connections.

Innovation, in the computerized age, turns into a device through which the family handles emergencies, offering new components of correspondence and backing. The assessment of how the family uses innovation during emergencies features its versatility and cleverness. Whether associating through virtual stages, planning emergency reaction endeavors, or looking for help on the web, innovation turns into a basic piece of the family's versatile systems, delineating how the advanced scene turns into an augmentation of familial strength.

The common memory of how the family handles emergencies through deliberate correspondence turns into a crucial part of emergency reaction. The assessment of how the family takes part in open exchanges, family gatherings, and purposeful conversations during emergencies uncovers a story of straightforward correspondence.

The family turns into a space where people feel appreciated, comprehended, and upheld, encouraging a culture of open correspondence that turns into a foundation of emergency goal and familial flexibility.

In the outcome of emergencies, the common memory of how the family considers the experience turns into an outline of aggregate development and change. The assessment of how the family processes examples learned, praises achievements of recuperation, and by and large offers thanks for the help got uncovers a story of versatility. The family turns into a material where the common experience of exploring emergencies adds to a story of development, reinforced familial bonds, and a more profound appreciation for the aggregate strength that arises in the midst of difficulty.

The idea of shared liabilities inside the family becomes essential to emergency reaction, stressing the significance of cooperative endeavors and common help. The assessment of how the family handles emergencies from the perspective of shared liabilities uncovers a story of aggregate critical thinking, asset designation, and a promise to bearing weights together. The family turns into a group where individual qualities join to explore difficulties, outlining the force of shared liabilities in supporting familial strength.

The common memory of how the family handles emergencies by encouraging a feeling of business as usual turns into an outline of its versatile limits and obligation to close to home prosperity. The assessment of how the family keeps up with schedules, makes snapshots of bliss in the midst of difficulties, and deliberately sustains a positive climate uncovers a story of strength and a pledge to safeguarding a feeling of predictability. The family turns into a safe-haven where empathy turns into an encouraging sign, adding to the profound balance of its individuals even amidst emergency.

The assessment of how the family handles emergencies through deliberate reflection turns into a story of aggregate contemplation, development, and a promise to nonstop improvement. Whether recognizing the illustrations got the hang of, praising achievements of recuperation, or by and large offering thanks for the help got, the family turns into a space where the common experience of exploring emergencies adds to a story of flexibility. Deliberate reflection turns into an extraordinary power, directing relatives toward a common future set apart by strength, understanding, and an extended appreciation for the securities that endure the trial of emergency.

The assessment of how the family handles emergencies disentangles a story that unpredictably winds around together the intricacies of misfortune and the groundbreaking influence of aggregate flexibility. From wellbeing emergencies and monetary difficulties to social struggles and outer disturbances, the family arises as a cauldron where caring reaction, open correspondence, and shared liabilities become essential to emergency goal.

The common memory of exploring emergencies turns into a demonstration of the getting through nature of familial bonds — a story that, even notwithstanding difficulty, enlightens the flexibility, strength, and enduring affection that characterize the familial excursion.

6.2 Stories of support and compassion during tough times.

In the many-sided embroidery of everyday life, the tales of help and sympathy during difficult stretches arise as strong stories that enlighten the strength, compassion, and interconnectedness of familial bonds. These accounts become encouraging signs, representing how the texture of family connections is woven with strings of faithful help and empathy, particularly when defied with difficulty.

One strong story unfurls during a wellbeing emergency, where a relative faces a difficult clinical conclusion. The aggregate reaction of the family turns into a demonstration of the strength tracked down in sympathy. From going with the person to innumerable clinical arrangements to holding vigils during medical clinic stays, the family frames a defensive circle, offering everyday reassurance and a feeling of having a place. The common memory of late-night discussions, shared tears, and giggling in the midst of vulnerability turns into a story of sympathy that rises above the limits of sickness, fashioning an aggregate excursion through the difficult stretches.

In another story, monetary difficulties cast a shadow over the family's security. Rather than surrendering to surrender, the family energizes together, changing difficult stretches into a common chance for joint effort and strength. Every part contributes their abilities, investigates new roads for money, and explores monetary imperatives aggregately. The common memory of adjusting to an easier way of life, focusing on needs over needs, and celebrating little monetary triumphs turns into a story of help, showing how empathy turns into a main thrust in changing difficulties into valuable open doors for shared development.

Misery, an unavoidable guest in the embroidery of life, meshes its direction into the family's story. In the tale of a critical misfortune, the relatives draw strength from each other, making a space for shared grieving and recognition. Empathy turns into the language of lamenting, with the family offering comfort, understanding, and an aggregate hug that recognizes the exceptional excursion of every part through the difficult stretches of deprivation. The common memory of remembrance administrations, flame lit vigils, and the formation of a family heritage project turns into a demonstration of the persevering through help that ties the family together even notwithstanding significant misfortune.

In the domain of individual emergencies, a story unfurls where a relative wrestles with character battles and emotional wellness challenges. Rather than staying away, the family turns into an unfaltering wellspring of adoration and acknowledgment.

The common memory of innumerable treatment meetings, open discussions, and the aggregate obligation to breaking down the shame encompassing psychological wellness turns into a story of empathy. The family changes difficult stretches into an excursion of figuring out, development, and shared versatility, representing how compassion turns into the foundation of familial help notwithstanding individual battles.

Outside emergencies, whether as cataclysmic events or cultural disturbances, become parts in the family's account of aggregate strength. In one story, a family faces the consequence of a cataclysmic event that upsets their lives. Rather than surrendering to surrender, the family use their common assets to reconstruct and uphold one another. The common memory of clearing flotsam and jetsam, remaking homes, and finding comfort in mutual endeavors turns into a story of empathy, outlining how difficult stretches become open doors for the family to reclassify their aggregate strength and solidarity.

Social emergencies, frequently many-sided and genuinely charged, track down goal through accounts of familial help and sympathy. In one such account, clashes emerge, testing the bonds that integrate relatives. Rather than allowing strife to rot, the family takes part in open correspondence, effectively pays attention to one another's viewpoints, and looks for goal through getting it. The common memory of family gatherings, genuine expressions of remorse, and the purposeful development of pardoning turns into an account of empathy that changes difficult stretches into an impetus for social development.

Sympathy and backing likewise manifest in accounts of instructive and vocation challenges. In a story of scholastic battles, a relative countenances misfortunes in their instructive excursion. The family answers not with judgment but rather with support, offering coaching, establishing a favorable report climate, and celebrating little triumphs. The common memory of late-night concentrate on meetings, conquering scholastic obstacles, and the family's aggregate obligation to instructive achievement turns into a story of relentless help, showing how difficult stretches become venturing stones for individual development inside the familial hug.

Innovation, in the computerized age, turns into a vital player in accounts of help during difficult stretches. In one story, relatives isolated by geological distances use innovation to overcome any barrier during an emergency. Video calls, virtual family social affairs, and online encouraging groups of people become life savers that rise above actual hindrances. The common memory of associating through screens, sharing updates continuously, and all in all exploring difficult stretches turns into an account of flexibility and versatility in the computerized time.

The assessment of accounts of help and empathy during difficult stretches likewise uncovers the meaning of deliberate correspondence inside the family. In testing minutes, the family participates in open exchanges, guaranteeing that every part feels appreciated, comprehended, and esteemed.

The common memory of purposeful discussions, undivided attention, and the formation of a space where weaknesses are embraced turns into a story of compassionate correspondence that sustains familial bonds notwithstanding difficulty.

Coordinated effort and shared liabilities arise as necessary topics in accounts of difficult stretches. In a story of monetary difficulties, the relatives join to explore monetary limitations and track down savvy fixes. Every part takes on liabilities, adds to shared objectives, and altogether endures the hardship. The common memory of monetary arranging meetings, asset designation, and the family's obligation to shared help turns into a story of shared liabilities that changes difficult stretches into open doors for aggregate critical thinking.

Keeping a feeling of business as usual turns into a strong story inside the family's account during difficult stretches. Despite challenges, the family deliberately makes snapshots of euphoria, jam schedules, and encourages a positive climate. The common memory of chuckling in the midst of hardships, shared feasts, and the deliberate development of a supporting environment turns into an account of strength. The family changes difficult stretches into a confirmation of their aggregate soul, outlining how a pledge to business as usual turns into a wellspring of solidarity and solidarity.

Reflection, both individual and group, turns into an extraordinary power in accounts of difficult stretches. The family carves out opportunity to recognize the illustrations learned, praise achievements of recuperation, and offer thanks for the help got. The common memory of family reflections turns into a story of development, flexibility, and an extended appreciation for the familial bonds that get through even despite difficulty. Difficult stretches become parts in a bigger story of familial development, outlining how reflection turns into a compass directing relatives toward a common future set apart by strength, understanding, and a significant feeling of association.

The accounts of help and sympathy during difficult stretches complicatedly wind around together the mind boggling embroidery of familial connections. From wellbeing emergencies and monetary difficulties to sorrow, individual battles, and outside disturbances, these accounts represent that difficult stretches become open doors for the family to rethink, reinforce, and commend their aggregate bonds. The common recollections of empathy, versatility, and steadfast help become strings that face the hardships of difficulty as well as add to the persevering through story of familial love — an account that rises above difficult stretches and resounds through the common heartbeat of the family.

6.3 Lessons learned from facing adversity together.

In the excursion of day to day life, confronting misfortune together turns into a pot that produces versatility, braces bonds, and gives significant examples.

These examples, carved into the aggregate account of familial connections, act as guideposts that enlighten the way toward strength, understanding, and shared development. As the family defies difficulties going from wellbeing emergencies to monetary misfortunes, sadness, and unexpected conditions, the illustrations learned become a necessary piece of the familial woven artwork.

One significant example unfurls even with a wellbeing emergency that contacts the existence of a relative. As the family revitalizes together, the illustration of solidarity and faithful help becomes the overwhelming focus. The common experience of going to clinical arrangements, offering close to home comfort, and exploring the intricacies of medical services imparts the comprehension that, notwithstanding wellbeing difficulty, solidarity turns into a guide of solidarity. The family discovers that confronting wellbeing challenges together offers useful help as well as develops a common flexibility that faces the hardship of vulnerability.

Monetary mishaps, one more type of difficulty, become a homeroom where the family learns the example of flexibility and joint effort. As every part contributes their abilities, investigates new roads for money, and aggregately explores monetary limitations, the family finds the influence of joint effort in beating monetary affliction. The example of flexibility turns into a mantra, directing the family to track down intelligent fixes, focus on needs, and celebrate even the littlest monetary triumphs. The common experience of monetary difficulties changes into an example that flexibility and versatility are innate characteristics that flourish when supported all in all.

Distress, an unavoidable guest in the human experience, meshes its own example into the familial account. Even with significant misfortune, the family finds the illustration of sympathy and the significance of making a space for shared grieving and recognition. The aggregate excursion through melancholy turns into an encapsulation of the illustration that compassion ties familial bonds significantly more tight during difficult stretches. The family discovers that recognizing individual pain, offering merciful help, and regarding the memory of friends and family make a story of getting through adoration that rises above the hardest snapshots of misfortune.

Individual emergencies, whether personality battles or emotional well-being difficulties, become homerooms where the family learns the illustration of unqualified acknowledgment and understanding. As one relative wrestles with individual difficulties, the illustration of sympathy unfurls. The family finds that offering genuine love, establishing a climate liberated from judgment, and participating in open discussions about emotional wellness encourage an air of acknowledgment. The common excursion through private emergencies turns into an illustration in embracing individual battles as a feature of the aggregate story, building up the comprehension that familial bonds blossom with genuine help.

Outside emergencies, whether as catastrophic events or cultural disturbances, become fields where the family learns the example of aggregate versatility and flexibility. In the result of outer difficulties, the family finds that the example of solidarity even with misfortune stretches out past its limits. The common experience of remaking, supporting each other through unanticipated difficulties, and effectively adding to local area recuperation turns into a demonstration of the example that aggregate flexibility reinforces familial bonds as well as waves outward, making a positive effect on the more extensive world.

Social emergencies, perplexing and sincerely charged, show the family the illustration of pardoning, open correspondence, and the ground-breaking force of recuperating. As clashes emerge, the family discovers that the example of deliberate correspondence turns into an impetus for goal. Open discoursed, undivided attention, and a guarantee to seeing each other's viewpoints become fundamental parts of the illustration in exploring social emergencies. The family finds that pardoning isn't just a gift to the excused yet additionally a type of self-freedom, adding to the example that recuperating changes difficult stretches into valuable open doors for social development.

In the domain of instructive and vocation challenges, the family learns the illustration of support, flexibility, and the force of celebrating individual triumphs. As a relative countenances difficulties in schooling or vocation, the aggregate reaction turns into an illustration in offering resolute help. The family finds that the illustration of celebrating little triumphs, giving support during mishaps, and cultivating a climate where every part's accomplishments are esteemed adds to a story of shared achievement. The family discovers that difficult stretches become open doors for individual development, and the aggregate emotionally supportive network turns into an establishment for strength.

Innovation, a huge player in the cutting edge familial scene, turns into a device through which the family learns the example of versatility and the force of virtual association. Even with difficulties that require topographical distance, the family finds that innovation turns into an extension. Virtual family get-togethers, online encouraging groups of people, and computerized correspondence diverts become illustrations in flexibility, demonstrating the way that familial bonds can flourish even in the virtual domain. That's what the family discovers, in the advanced age, innovation turns into an expansion of familial help, giving roads to association and shared encounters during difficult stretches.

The assessment of illustrations gained from confronting misfortune together likewise uncovers the example of deliberate correspondence. In testing minutes, the family participates in open exchanges, guaranteeing that every part feels appreciated, comprehended, and esteemed. The common experience of deliberate discussions turns into an illustration in making a space where weaknesses are embraced. The family discovers that the example of purposeful correspondence turns into a foundation of emergency goal, encouraging a climate where sympathy and grasping prosper.

Cooperation and shared liabilities arise as basic topics in the illustrations gained from confronting difficulty together. Even with monetary difficulties, the relatives join to explore monetary requirements and track down clever fixes. The example of shared liabilities turns into a story of aggregate critical thinking, representing how every part's commitment reinforces the familial emotionally supportive network. The family discovers that the illustration of cooperation changes difficult stretches into amazing open doors for shared development, supporting that the aggregate strength of the family is more prominent than the amount of its singular parts.

Keeping a feeling of predictability turns into a piercing example inside the family's story during difficult stretches. Notwithstanding challenges, the family deliberately makes snapshots of bliss, jam schedules, and cultivates a positive climate. The illustration of saving business as usual turns into a wellspring of solidarity and solidarity. The family discovers that the illustration of keeping a feeling of business as usual, even amidst difficulty, adds to the close to home balance of its individuals and turns into a demonstration of their aggregate soul.

Reflection, both individual and group, turns into an extraordinary illustration in the repercussions of emergencies. The family finds opportunity to recognize the examples learned, praise achievements of recuperation, and offer thanks for the help got. The common memory of family reflections turns into an example in development, strength, and an extended appreciation for the familial bonds that persevere through even despite difficulty. Difficult stretches become sections in a bigger story of familial development, outlining how reflection turns into a compass directing relatives toward a common future set apart by strength, understanding, and a significant feeling of association.

Inside the story of familial bonds manufactured in the cauldron of misfortune, a significant example arises — the illustration of appreciation. As the family ponders the difficulties confronted and the aggregate excursion through difficult stretches, appreciation turns into a core value that shapes their point of view and improves their common story.

Following wellbeing emergencies, the example of appreciation flourishes as the relatives express significant appreciation for the endowment of wellbeing and the flexibility of their friends and family. The common memory of emergency clinic stays, clinical medicines, and the close to home rollercoaster of vulnerability turns into a story of appreciation for every day of prosperity. The family discovers that the example of appreciation reaches out past the actual difficulties, saturating regular daily existence with an increased consciousness of the value of wellbeing and the interconnectedness of their prosperity.

Monetary difficulties, while requesting and extraordinary, become a ripe ground for the example of appreciation. The family figures out how to see the value in the worth of genius, imaginative critical thinking, and the flexibility that arises even with financial difficulty.

The common memory of fixing spending plans, tracking down satisfaction in straightforwardness, and all in all exploring monetary vulnerabilities turns into a story of appreciation for the examples learned in overseeing assets carefully. The family finds that the example of appreciation reaches out to the overflow found in shared encounters and the strength got from enduring monetary tempests together.

In the reverberations of despondency and misfortune, the example of appreciation appears as the family treasures the recollections of friends and family and recognizes the significant effect of shared grieving. The aggregate excursion through difficult stretches turns into a story of appreciation for the love that perseveres through even past the actual presence of the individuals who have passed. The family discovers that the example of appreciation reaches out to the tradition of esteemed minutes, the strength drawn from shared grieving, and the getting through bond that rises above the limits of life and passing.

Individual emergencies, set apart by character battles or emotional wellness challenges, become domains where the example of appreciation unfurls. The family figures out how to see the value in the strength tracked down in weakness, the extraordinary force of unrestricted acknowledgment, and the magnificence of individual development. The common memory of open discussions, treatment meetings, and the deliberate development of an air of acknowledgment turns into a story of appreciation for the uniqueness of every relative's excursion. The family finds that the illustration of appreciation reaches out to the lavishness tracked down in embracing the intricacies of distinction and the common obligation to cultivating a climate of unrestricted love.

Outer emergencies, whether as cataclysmic events or cultural disturbances, become parts where the illustration of appreciation becomes the dominant focal point. The family figures out how to see the value in the versatility that surfaces in aggregate endeavors to remake, support, and add to local area recuperation. The common experience of confronting outer difficulties turns into a story of appreciation for the interconnectedness of their lives with the more extensive world. The family finds that the example of appreciation reaches out to the attention to their aggregate effect and the significance of effectively adding to the prosperity of the networks they are essential for.

Social emergencies, complicated and sincerely charged, become fields where the example of appreciation unfurls through pardoning, understanding, and the extraordinary force of recuperating. The family figures out how to see the value in the strength found in pardoning, the profundity of understanding that arises through open correspondence, and the magnificence of social development. The common memory of family gatherings, sincere statements of regret, and the deliberate development of pardoning turns into a story of appreciation for the versatility of familial securities. The family finds that the example of appreciation stretches out to the limit with respect to restoration, the affirmation of shared blemishes, and the obligation to sustaining associations with compassion and understanding.

In the domain of instructive and profession challenges, the illustration of appreciation surfaces as the family values the common triumphs, regardless of how little, and the strength got from shared consolation. The family figures out how to be thankful for the chances to celebrate individual accomplishments, to offer unflinching help during difficulties, and to encourage a climate where every part's development is esteemed. The common memory of conquering instructive obstacles, exploring profession mishaps, and the family's aggregate obligation to shared achievement turns into a story of appreciation for the excursion of individual and aggregate headway.

Innovation, an essential piece of the cutting edge familial scene, turns into a course for the illustration of appreciation. The family figures out how to see the value in the job of innovation in encouraging virtual associations during seasons of geological distance. The common experience of video calls, virtual family social events, and the utilization of computerized stages for help turns into a story of appreciation for the manners in which innovation upgrades familial associations. The family finds that the example of appreciation reaches out to the versatility worked with by innovation and the wealth found in remaining associated, in any event, when actual distances present difficulties.

Purposeful correspondence, a foundation in the familial reaction to difficult stretches, turns into an example in appreciation. The family figures out how to see the value in the force of open exchanges, undivided attention, and the making of a space where every part's voice is heard. The common memory of deliberate discussions turns into a story of appreciation for the strength tracked down in straightforward correspondence. The family finds that the illustration of appreciation stretches out to the developed grasping, fortified securities, and the persevering through help that blooms when deliberate correspondence turns into a core value.

Cooperation and shared liabilities, basic subjects in the familial reaction to challenges, become an illustration in appreciation. The family figures out how to see the value in the aggregate critical thinking, the dispersion of assignments, and the common obligation to enduring tempests together. The common memory of exploring difficulties as a group turns into a story of appreciation for the strength got from shared liabilities. The family finds that the illustration of appreciation stretches out to the acknowledgment that the aggregate strength of the family is a repository of help that outperforms individual limits.

Keeping a feeling of business as usual, an impactful illustration in familial reaction to difficult stretches, turns into an example in appreciation.

The family figures out how to see the value in the snapshots of delight, the safeguarding of schedules, and the purposeful development of a positive climate. The common memory of chuckling in the midst of hardships, shared feasts, and the purposeful work to make predictability turns into a story of appreciation for the versatility that arises despite misfortune.

The family finds that the example of appreciation reaches out to the affirmation that, even in difficult stretches, there is an abundance of shared minutes that add to the close to home harmony of its individuals.

Reflection, both individual and group, turns into a groundbreaking example in appreciation. The family finds opportunity to recognize the examples learned, commend achievements of recuperation, and offer thanks for the help got. The common memory of family reflections turns into a story of appreciation for the development, strength, and extended appreciation for the familial bonds that get through even notwithstanding misfortune. Difficult stretches become parts in a bigger story of familial development, representing how reflection turns into a compass directing relatives toward a common future set apart by strength, understanding, and a significant feeling of association.

The example of appreciation unpredictably winds around together the complicated embroidery of familial connections. From wellbeing emergencies and monetary difficulties to pain, individual battles, and outside disturbances, this example shows that difficult stretches become open doors for the family to develop a profound feeling of appreciation for the lavishness tracked down in shared encounters. The common recollections of appreciation become strings that face the hardships of difficulty as well as add to the getting through story of familial love — a story that rises above difficult stretches and resounds through the common heartbeat of the family.

Chapter 7

"Legacy of Love"

In the significant embroidery of familial connections, the "Tradition of Adoration" arises as an immortal story that rises above ages, winds through shared encounters, and turns into a directing light through the different sections of everyday life. This heritage isn't just an assortment of recollections however a no nonsense demonstration of the persevering through strength, flexibility, and interconnectedness of the familial bond. As the family explores the complex dance of life's victories and difficulties, the tradition of affection turns into a primary string that ties past, present, and future into a consistent continuum.

The tradition of affection unfurls through the everyday ceremonies and shared minutes that make the heartbeat of familial connections. Whether it's the glow of a common dinner, the chuckling that reverberations through the corridors, or the calm snapshots of understanding, these encounters become the brushstrokes that paint the representation of the family's heritage. The tradition of adoration is found in fantastic motions as well as in the little, regular thoughtful gestures, the predictable presence of help, and the faithful obligation to one another's prosperity.

As the family faces wellbeing emergencies, the tradition of affection uncovers itself as a wellspring of comfort, strength, and steadfast help. At the point when a relative wrestles with sickness, the tradition of adoration turns into a shelter — changing lounge areas into spaces loaded up with shared stories, emergency clinic visits into articulations of care, and the vulnerability of clinical determinations into valuable open doors for aggregate versatility. The tradition of adoration sparkles most splendid at these times, showing that familial bonds become a strong wellspring of mending and that adoration, when shared, has the ability to rise above the limits of actual difficulties.

Monetary difficulties, while testing the family's fortitude, become a field where the tradition of affection fashions a way of cooperation, genius, and shared liability. As the family faces the hardship of monetary vulnerabilities, the tradition of adoration is obvious in the common endeavors to find effective fixes, the penances made for a long term benefit, and the festival of even the littlest monetary triumphs. The tradition of affection instructs that familial bonds are a wellspring of solidarity, offering an emotionally supportive network that stretches out past money related concerns and reaffirming that affection is a cash that enhances the aggregate soul.

In snapshots of distress and misfortune, the tradition of affection turns into an encouraging hug — a common space where grieving is met with understanding, and the aggravation of misfortune is relaxed by the aggregate strength of familial bonds. The family's tradition of affection isn't quenched by the progression of time; all things being equal, it turns into a reference point of light during the most obscure hours, encouraging a climate where recollections are treasured, and the getting through effect of friends and family is praised. The tradition of affection exhibits that even notwithstanding significant misfortune, the familial bond turns into a safe-haven of sympathy, delineating that affection has the influence to rise above the limits between the living and the left.

As private emergencies unfurl inside the family, the tradition of affection turns into an example in acknowledgment, sympathy, and the festival of distinction. Whether a relative wrestles with character battles, psychological wellness difficulties, or individual vulnerabilities, the tradition of affection instructs that familial bonds give a relentless groundwork of acknowledgment and backing. The family's tradition of affection turns into a demonstration of the comprehension that every part is exceptional, that weaknesses are embraced, and that adoration has the groundbreaking ability to support self-awareness inside the familial hug.

Outside emergencies, whether cataclysmic events or cultural disturbances, become sections in the family's tradition of adoration, featuring the significance of aggregate versatility and a guarantee to local area. As the family faces outside difficulties, the tradition of affection is appeared in the common endeavors to reconstruct, support neighbors, and add to the more extensive prosperity of society. The family discovers that adoration isn't restricted to its own limits however expands outward, making a far reaching influence of empathy and positive effect.

The tradition of affection exhibits that familial bonds are entwined with a more extensive feeling of obligation and a common obligation to having a constructive outcome on the planet.

In the domain of social emergencies, the tradition of adoration shows the groundbreaking force of pardoning, open correspondence, and the obligation to supporting solid connections. At the point when clashes emerge, the family's tradition of adoration turns into a directing light, enlightening the way toward figuring out, mending, and the deliberate development of pardoning. The tradition of affection is clear in the family's obligation to undivided attention, helpful discourse, and the flexibility that permits familial bonds to weather conditions even the most difficult social tempests.

Instructive and vocation challenges, while introducing obstacles, become fields where the tradition of affection gives the example of support, versatility, and shared achievement. As relatives explore difficulties and accomplishments in training and profession pursuits, the tradition of affection turns into a story of steady help, celebrating individual triumphs, and cultivating a climate where every part's development is esteemed. The family discovers that adoration isn't just a wellspring of daily reassurance yet additionally an impetus for individual and aggregate progression, molding a heritage that urges every part to arrive at their fullest potential.

In the computerized age, innovation turns into a device through which the tradition of affection is communicated and supported, crossing over geological distances and cultivating virtual associations. Whether through video calls, virtual family social occasions, or online encouraging groups of people, innovation turns into an expansion of the family's tradition of adoration. The family discovers that adoration isn't restricted by actual limits and that innovation turns into a conductor for remaining associated, sharing encounters, and supporting familial bonds, even notwithstanding distance.

Deliberate correspondence, a foundation in the family's reaction to challenges, turns into an illustration in the tradition of adoration. The family discovers that open exchanges, undivided attention, and the making of a space where every part feels appreciated are essential to the statement of adoration. The tradition of adoration turns into a story of compassionate correspondence, showing that understanding is developed through deliberate discussions, and that adoration isn't just an inclination yet a continuous discourse that shapes the familial account.

Joint effort and shared liabilities, basic subjects in the familial reaction to challenges, become an example in the tradition of adoration. The family discovers that adoration isn't uninvolved yet effectively communicated through shared critical thinking, the circulation of undertakings, and an aggregate obligation to enduring tempests together. The tradition of affection instructs that familial bonds are fortified through shared liabilities, building up the possibility that the aggregate strength of the family is more prominent than the amount of its singular parts.

Keeping a feeling of business as usual turns into a strong example inside the family's story during difficult stretches, and the tradition of affection turns into a core value in protecting schedules, making snapshots of satisfaction, and encouraging a good climate. The family discovers that adoration is a balancing out force, permitting them to explore difficulties with strength, track down bliss in the midst of troubles, and develop a feeling of predictability that turns into a demonstration of their aggregate soul.

Reflection, both individual and group, turns into an extraordinary power in the tradition of adoration. The family finds opportunity to recognize the illustrations learned, commend achievements of recuperation, and offer thanks for the help got. The common memory of family reflections turns into a story of development, strength, and an extended appreciation for the familial bonds that persevere through even despite misfortune. Difficult stretches become sections in a bigger story of familial development, delineating how reflection turns into a compass directing relatives toward a common future set apart by strength, understanding, and a significant feeling of association.

As the family's process unfurls, the tradition of adoration turns into an immortal story that winds through the mind boggling strings of familial connections. It is a story composed not in ink but rather in the common encounters, the steadfast help, and the getting through responsibility that characterize the familial bond. The tradition of adoration rises above the limits of time, making a story that reverberations through ages, molding the personality of the family and turning into a wellspring of motivation for the individuals who follow. An inheritance reminds every relative that they are important for something more noteworthy — a whole chain of affection that ties past, present, and future into an embroidery of getting through strength and association. The tradition of affection isn't simply a story; it is a no nonsense demonstration of the force of familial bonds — a heritage that keeps on unfurling as time passes, shaping the family's story with the immortal elegance of getting through affection.

7.1 Reflection on the family's journey.

In the calm snapshots of reflection, the family winds up at the junction of its aggregate process — an excursion woven with strings of shared encounters, versatility, delight, challenges, and an immovable obligation to one another. This intelligent interruption turns into a potential chance to follow the forms of the family's story, to see the value in the embroidered artwork of minutes that have molded its character, and to draw illustrations from the parts that have unfurled.

As the family considers its excursion, a piercing subject that arises is the extraordinary force of fellowship. Through wellbeing emergencies, monetary difficulties, individual battles, and outside disturbances, the family finds that its solidarity lies in solidarity. The aggregate reaction to moves turns into a demonstration of the interconnectedness of familial securities, showing that confronting misfortune together isn't simply a method for surviving yet a wellspring of significant strength.

In the reflection on wellbeing emergencies, the family perceives that the common excursion through clinical vulnerabilities brought them closer, cultivating a feeling of shared help and compassion that became essential to their aggregate character.

The reflection stretches out to snapshots of monetary test, where the family took in the specialty of cooperation, genius, and shared liability. The common experience of exploring monetary imperatives and finding clever fixes turns into a story of aggregate critical thinking. The family comprehends that monetary difficulties were not just impediments however open doors for development, showing them the worth of versatility and the strength got from enduring financial tempests together. As they ponder these minutes, the family understands that the tradition of harmony is a foundation of their excursion — a heritage that rises above individual victories and disappointments.

Despite misery and misfortune, the family's appearance develops into the comprehension that common grieving is a significant articulation of affection. The aggregate reaction to misfortune turns into a story of sympathy, where the family makes a space for recognition, values the traditions of left friends and family, and explores the floods of sorrow with shared strength. The reflection on these minutes uncovers that, even in the profundities of distress, the family found a persevering through security — a security that rises above the limits of life and turns into a demonstration of the versatility of adoration.

Individual emergencies, frequently multifaceted and profoundly private, become accounts of win inside the family's intelligent look. The excursion through personality battles, psychological well-being difficulties, and individual vulnerabilities turns into a story of acknowledgment and development. The family ponders the examples learned — the significance of genuine love, the force of sympathy, and the magnificence tracked down in praising singularity. These reflections shape the comprehension that the family's process is stamped by aggregate victories as well as by the strength drawn from embracing the uniqueness of every part's way.

Outside emergencies, whether as cataclysmic events or cultural disturbances, become sections in the family's appearance on its excursion. The common endeavors to reconstruct, support networks, and add to more extensive prosperity become a demonstration of the family's feeling of obligation past its own limits. The reflection develops into a mindfulness that the family isn't confined yet interconnected with a world that has comparative difficulties and delights. The family discovers that its process is entwined with a more extensive story of mankind, and the tradition of aggregate liability turns into a core value in exploring the intricacies of an interconnected world.

Social emergencies, set apart by clashes and difficulties, become reflections on absolution, understanding, and the groundbreaking force of mending. As the family ponders snapshots of friction, it perceives the significance of purposeful correspondence, undivided attention, and the obligation to encouraging solid connections.

The reflection on social difficulties uncovers that pardoning isn't a shortcoming however a strength — a strength that permits the family to push ahead, become together, and develop the bonds that have endured everyday hardship.

Instructive and vocation challenges, as the family thinks back, become accounts of consolation, shared achievement, and the satisfaction got from every part's development. The family ponders the illustrations bestowed — the meaning of help, the festival of individual triumphs, and the affirmation that every part's process adds to the aggregate story. These reflections shape the comprehension that the family's process is set apart by a guarantee to shared achievement, where individual accomplishments are private victories as well as aggregate triumphs that enhance the familial character.

In the computerized age, innovation turns into a reflection on versatility and the force of virtual association. The family perceives that innovation, when utilized deliberately, turns into a scaffold that traverses topographical distances and cultivates associations in the computerized domain. The reflection on these minutes highlights the significance of remaining associated, sharing encounters, and supporting familial bonds through the developing scene of innovation. That's what the family discovers, in the reflection on its computerized venture, innovation isn't a hindrance yet a device that upgrades the interconnectedness of its individuals.

Deliberate correspondence, a foundation in the family's reaction to challenges, turns into a reflection on the profundity of understanding that arises through open discoursed. The family ponders the snapshots of straightforward correspondence, perceiving that purposeful discussions make a space where weaknesses are embraced, false impressions are explained, and love is communicated in words as well as in the deliberate demonstration of tuning in. The reflection uncovers that the family's process is molded by a pledge to compassionate correspondence — a responsibility that braces familial bonds.

Cooperation and shared liabilities, major subjects in the familial reaction to challenges, become reflections on the force of aggregate critical thinking. As the family thinks back on snapshots of shared liabilities, it perceives that joint effort isn't simply a functional need however an impression of the common obligation to enduring tempests together. The reflection on shared liabilities develops into a comprehension that the family's process is set apart by the aggregate strength got from every part's commitment, building up the possibility that the amount of their endeavors outperforms individual limits.

Keeping a feeling of business as usual turns into a powerful reflection inside the family's story during difficult stretches. The deliberate making of snapshots of euphoria, the protection of schedules, and the cultivating of a positive climate become reflections on the strength that arises even with difficulty. The family ponders the comprehension that, even in difficult stretches, there is an abundance of shared minutes that add to the profound balance of its individuals. The reflection on keeping a feeling of business as usual turns into a demonstration of the family's obligation to developing euphoria in the midst of challenges.

Reflection, both individual and group, turns into a groundbreaking power in the outcome of emergencies. The family finds opportunity to recognize the examples learned, praise achievements of recuperation, and offer thanks for the help got. The reflection on family reflections turns into a story of development, strength, and an extended appreciation for the familial bonds that persevere through even notwithstanding misfortune. The family comprehends that difficult stretches become parts in a bigger story of familial development — a story molded by reflection, strength, and a common vision for what's to come.

As the family's process unfurls in the intelligent look, the tradition of adoration arises as a focal subject — a heritage that envelops the ups and downs, the victories and difficulties, and the aggregate strength that ties past, present, and future. The reflection on the tradition of adoration uncovers that familial bonds are not static yet unique, advancing with each insight, challenge, and win. The family discovers that the tradition of affection isn't simply a memory however a no nonsense story that keeps on forming its personality with the immortal elegance of getting through adoration.

All in all, the family's appearance on its process turns into a rich embroidery woven with strings of fellowship, strength, understanding, and love. The account of wellbeing emergencies, monetary difficulties, individual battles, and outside disturbances uncovers that the family's solidarity lies in solidarity, and its process is set apart by the groundbreaking force of confronting misfortune together. The reflection on snapshots of pain, individual emergencies, and social difficulties shows that the family's heritage isn't characterized by flawlessness however by the obligation to pardoning, understanding, and the groundbreaking force of recuperating.

Instructive and profession challenges become reflections on shared achievement, consolation, and the festival of individual development. The family's computerized venture turns into a reflection on versatility and the force of innovation to improve familial associations. Deliberate correspondence, cooperation, and shared liabilities become reflections on the profundity of understanding that arises through straightforward exchange and the aggregate strength got from every part's commitment. Keeping a feeling of predictability turns into an impactful reflection on the strength that arises even despite misfortune.

At last, reflection turns into a compass directing the family toward a common future set apart by development, understanding, and a significant feeling of association. The family's process is definitely not a straight way yet a nuanced story, molded by the rhythmic movement of encounters, the illustrations drawn from difficulties, and the persevering through tradition of affection that ties ages together. In the intelligent respite, the family finds that its process isn't simply a progression of occasions yet a living, developing story — a story composed with the permanent ink of fellowship and love — a story that keeps on unfurling with the commitment of new sections and shared skylines.

Inside the rich embroidered artwork of the family's appearance on its excursion, the account develops into an investigation of strength — a complicated string that winds through the ups and downs, characterizing the family's reaction to difficulties and molding its aggregate personality.

As the family ponders snapshots of difficulty, the subject of flexibility turns into a core value — a wellspring of solidarity that rises above individual battles and impels the family forward with unflinching assurance.

Notwithstanding wellbeing emergencies, the family's appearance divulges the significant flexibility that surfaces when defied with the delicacy of prosperity. The common experience of clinical vulnerabilities turns into a story of strength, showing that the family's reaction to wellbeing challenges is set apart by flexibility, fortitude, and an aggregate obligation to supporting each other. The reflection on wellbeing emergencies instructs that versatility isn't simply a response to hardships however a proactive power — an inward strength that empowers the family to explore the intricacies of medical care with elegance and determination.

Monetary difficulties, frequently seen as overwhelming hindrances, become reflections on the family's financial strength. As the family ponders snapshots of monetary vulnerability, it perceives that versatility isn't only about enduring monetary tempests however about tracking down intelligent fixes, adjusting to evolving conditions, and encouraging a feeling of aggregate liability. The family's monetary excursion turns into a demonstration of the versatility got from coordinated effort, creativity, and a common obligation to defeating financial difficulties. The reflection on monetary flexibility uncovers that, even despite money related vulnerabilities, the family arises more grounded, more ingenious, and better prepared to explore future monetary scenes.

Melancholy and misfortune, significant and extraordinary, become reflections on the strength that arises right after personal disturbance. The common experience of grieving turns into a story of flexibility, representing that the family's reaction to misfortune is set apart by shared help, recognition, and a getting through association with the recollections of left friends and family. The reflection on sadness instructs that versatility isn't tied in with smothering feelings yet about embracing them, tracking down comfort in shared grieving, and permitting the aggregate strength of familial bonds to be a wellspring of solace and recuperating.

Individual emergencies, set apart by character battles or psychological wellness challenges, become reflections on the strength that surfaces while confronting unseen conflicts. The family discovers that strength isn't just about returning quickly from hardships yet about cultivating a climate where weaknesses are recognized, and individual development is upheld. The common experience of exploring individual emergencies turns into a story of strength, showing that the family's reaction is set apart by sympathy, unrestricted love, and a promise to understanding and supporting every part's exceptional excursion. The reflection on private strength uncovers that, even despite inside difficulties, the family turns into a safe-haven of acknowledgment and development.

Outside emergencies, whether as cataclysmic events or cultural disturbances, become reflections on the flexibility that arises in the aggregate reaction to outer difficulties.

The family perceives that flexibility isn't simply a singular characteristic yet a common limit that surfaces while confronting more extensive vulnerabilities. The reflection on outside emergencies instructs that versatility isn't about disconnection yet about meeting up, adding to local area recuperation, and perceiving the interconnectedness of the family's excursion with the bigger world. That's what the family discovers, even despite outer difficulties, its aggregate versatility turns into a power for positive change and local area influence.

Social emergencies, multifaceted and genuinely charged, become reflections on the strength that arises through absolution, understanding, and the obligation to supporting sound connections. The family understands that versatility in connections isn't tied in with staying away from clashes yet about exploring them with elegance and receptiveness. The common experience of conquering social difficulties turns into a story of versatility, showing that the family's reaction is set apart by purposeful correspondence, pardoning, and the groundbreaking force of mending. The reflection on social flexibility uncovers that, even notwithstanding clashes, the family turns into a demonstration of the getting through strength of its bonds.

Instructive and profession challenges, frequently seen as obstacles, become reflections on the flexibility that surfaces chasing after individual and aggregate development. The family perceives that strength isn't just about intellectual or expert accomplishments however about offering steady help during misfortunes, celebrating individual triumphs, and cultivating a climate where every part's instructive and profession venture is esteemed. The reflection on instructive and profession flexibility uncovers that, even notwithstanding difficulties, the family turns into a wellspring of support, versatility, and shared achievement.

Innovation, a basic piece of the cutting edge familial scene, turns into a reflection on the strength expected to adjust to a quickly impacting computerized world. The family discovers that versatility isn't just about exploring innovative progressions yet about utilizing innovation deliberately to upgrade familial associations. The reflection on innovation strength uncovers that, even despite advanced difficulties, the family becomes capable at utilizing innovation to remain associated, share encounters, and sustain its bonds across geological distances.

Deliberate correspondence, a foundation in the familial reaction to challenges, turns into a reflection on the strength that arises through straightforward discourse. The family discovers that flexibility in correspondence isn't tied in with keeping away from troublesome discussions yet about making a space where every part's voice is heard, and understanding is developed. The reflection on correspondence strength uncovers that, even despite false impressions, the family becomes skilled at cultivating open exchanges, developing its comprehension, and sustaining its securities through purposeful correspondence.

Joint effort and shared liabilities, basic subjects in the familial reaction to challenges, become reflections on the versatility that surfaces in aggregate critical thinking. The family perceives that flexibility isn't simply a singular quality yet an aggregate strength that arises while confronting shared liabilities.

The reflection on joint effort strength uncovers that, even despite difficulties, the family turns into a strong unit, dispersing errands, and enduring tempests together. The family discovers that its common obligations become a pot for strength, manufacturing bonds that endure everyday hardship.

Keeping a feeling of business as usual, a powerful appearance in the familial reaction to difficult stretches, turns into an example in flexibility. The family understands that flexibility isn't just about getting through hardships however about deliberately making snapshots of bliss, protecting schedules, and encouraging a positive climate. The reflection on business as usual flexibility uncovers that, even notwithstanding difficulty, the family becomes skilled at tracking down happiness in the midst of troubles and developing a feeling of predictability that turns into a demonstration of its aggregate soul.

Reflection, both individual and group, turns into an extraordinary power in the result of emergencies, showing the family that flexibility isn't simply a response to moves yet a continuous obligation to development, understanding, and the persevering through strength of familial bonds. The family carves out opportunity to recognize the examples learned, commend achievements of recuperation, and offer thanks for the help got. The reflection on family reflections turns into a story of development, flexibility, and an extended appreciation for the familial bonds that persevere through even notwithstanding misfortune.

The family's appearance on its process turns into a significant investigation of flexibility — a topic that reverberations through snapshots of wellbeing emergencies, monetary difficulties, sadness, individual battles, outside disturbances, social contentions, instructive and vocation obstacles, innovative changes, purposeful correspondence, coordinated effort, shared liabilities, and the quest for business as usual. The reflection uncovers that strength is definitely not a latent quality yet a functioning power that shapes the family's reaction to challenges, braces its bonds, and turns into a core value chasing shared development and understanding. That's what the family discovers, in the embroidered artwork of its excursion, flexibility is the brilliant string that enlightens the way ahead, reminding every part that, together, they can beat any test and arise more grounded, savvier, and more joined than any other time in recent memory.

7.2 Consideration of the legacy passed down through generations.

As the family leaves on an insightful excursion through the chronicles of its common history, the thought of inheritance turns into a focal topic — an embroidery woven with the strings of customs, values, intelligence, and aggregate encounters that have been gone down through ages. The investigation of heritage isn't just a review look however a nuanced comprehension of the legacy that shapes the family's personality, convictions, and the manner in which it explores the embroidery of life.

Customs, woven into the texture of the family's inheritance, stand as ageless markers of progression. As the family considers the ceremonies, festivities, and customs that have persevered through the progression of time, it perceives that customs are not static however unique — a living articulation of shared values. The tradition of customs turns into a guidepost, giving a feeling of association with the past and offering a guide for people in the future. The family discovers that customs are ceremonies as well as stories that span ages, making a feeling of having a place and progression that rises above the limits of time.

Values, profoundly imbued in the family's heritage, arise as mainstays of solidarity that maintain the familial construction. The family ponders the moral standards, moral establishments, and shared convictions that have been gone down through the ages. The thought of values uncovers that they are not simple deliberations but rather living rules that shape the family's direction, connections, and aggregate personality. The family discovers that values are not forced yet embraced — a legacy that gives an ethical compass to exploring the intricacies of the world. In the reflection on values, the family finds that the heritage passed down isn't simply a bunch of standards however a supply of solidarity that sustains the familial bond.

Shrewdness, refined through the pot of involvement, turns into an important part of the family's heritage. The family ponders the examples took in, the tales shared, and the pearls of shrewdness passed down from older folks to more youthful ages. The thought of intelligence uncovers that it isn't simply information yet a no nonsense element that develops with every age. The family discovers that shrewdness isn't restricted to progress in years yet courses through the shared perspective, molding choices, cultivating flexibility, and giving an establishment to development. In the reflection on shrewdness, the family perceives that the heritage passed down isn't simply a storehouse of illustrations yet a wellspring of direction that enhances the familial story.

Aggregate encounters, carved into the family's heritage, become stories that tight spot ages together. As the family ponders shared wins, difficulties, and achievements, it perceives that the aggregate encounters are not disconnected occurrences but rather sections in a bigger story. The thought of aggregate encounters uncovers that they are recollections as well as strings that wind through the familial embroidery, making a feeling of solidarity and progression. The family discovers that common encounters are stories as well as a common heartbeat that reverberates through time, interfacing past, present, and people in the future. In the reflection on aggregate encounters, the family finds that the heritage passed down isn't simply a progression of occasions however a living story that shapes its character with the immortal elegance of shared history.

The passing down of inheritance turns into a purposeful demonstration, a deliberate transmission of values, customs, insight, and encounters starting with one age then onto the next.

The family considers the meaning of this intergenerational move, perceiving that it's anything but a one-way process yet a complementary trade that enhances both the provider and the beneficiary. In the thought of heritage transmission, the family discovers that it isn't just about safeguarding the past however about effectively forming what's in store. The family comprehends that the heritage passed down is certainly not a static legacy however a powerful power that develops with every age, adding to the continuous story of familial character.

The tradition of customs, as the family digs further into its appearance, uncovers itself as a scaffold between ages — a whole chain that joins progenitors, elderly folks, and relatives. The family considers the ceremonies that have been dependably noticed, the festivals that have reverberated as the years progressed, and the traditions that have turned into a sacrosanct piece of its personality. In the thought of customs, the family discovers that they are not relics of the past but rather living articulations of shared values and a demonstration of the persevering through strength of familial bonds. The family ponders how customs act as standards, cultivating a feeling of congruity, ingraining an association with roots, and making a common language that rises above fleeting limits.

Values, at the center of the family's inheritance, arise as directing stars that explore the familial excursion through evolving scenes. The family considers the moral rules that have endured over the extreme long haul, the ethical compass that has controlled choices, and the common convictions that have framed the groundwork of its character. In the thought of values, the family discovers that they are not static creeds but rather versatile rules that develop with the moving tides of society. The family ponders how values become a wellspring of strength, giving a system to moral direction, cultivating solidarity in variety, and shaping the family's reaction to challenges. In the reflection on values, the family comprehends that the heritage passed down isn't simply a bunch of standards however a unique power that shapes its personality and characterizes the aggregate ethos.

Shrewdness, as a crucial part of the family's heritage, unfurls as an embroidery woven with the strings of involvement, reflection, and shared bits of knowledge. The family considers the examples learned through preliminaries and wins, the narratives that convey the refined insight of older folks, and the pearls of understanding that have been gone down through ages. In the thought of shrewdness, the family discovers that it isn't bound to mature however courses through the shared mindset, molding choices, encouraging strength, and giving an establishment to development. The family ponders how shrewdness turns into a wellspring of coherence, interfacing the past with the present, and offering a signal of direction for what's to come. In the reflection on shrewdness, the family comprehends that the heritage passed down isn't simply a vault of information however a living power that enhances its story with profundity and smarts.

Aggregate encounters, entwined into the family's inheritance, arise as stories that tight spot ages together. The family ponders the common victories that have become wellsprings of motivation, the difficulties that have tried its strength, and the achievements that imprint its process through time. In the thought of aggregate encounters, the family discovers that they are not segregated occurrences but rather sections in a bigger story — a story that rises above individual lives and makes a common feeling of personality. The family ponders how aggregate encounters become a common heartbeat, reverberating through time and interfacing the strings of its story. In the reflection on aggregate encounters, the family comprehends that the heritage passed down isn't simply a progression of occasions yet a living story that shapes its character with the immortal effortlessness of shared history.

Heritage transmission, as the family mulls over its deliberate passing down, turns into a significant demonstration of association between ages. The family thinks about the purposeful work to move values, customs, intelligence, and aggregate encounters from older folks to more youthful individuals. In the thought of heritage transmission, the family discovers that it isn't simply an exchange of information however a corresponding trade that improves both the provider and the beneficiary. The family considers how purposeful inheritance transmission turns into a scaffold between the insight of the past and the capability representing things to come, encouraging a feeling of congruity and guaranteeing that the familial story stays energetic and important. In the reflection on heritage transmission, the family comprehends that the demonstration of passing down heritage is definitely not a one-time event however a consistent exchange that shapes the continuous story of familial character.

The reflection on the heritage went down through ages turns into a chance for the family to participate in a discourse with own story — a thoughtful investigation develops how its might interpret the qualities, customs, shrewdness, and aggregate encounters that structure the underpinning of its personality. As the family considers the tradition of customs, it remembers them as social relics as well as living articulations of shared values and a demonstration of the getting through strength of familial bonds. The family considers how customs act as standards, cultivating a feeling of progression, ingraining an association with roots, and making a common language that rises above transient limits.

Values, at the center of the family's heritage, arise as directing stars that explore the familial excursion through evolving scenes. The family thinks about the moral rules that have endured over the extreme long haul, the ethical compass that has directed choices, and the common convictions that have shaped the groundwork of its character. In the thought of values, the family discovers that they are not static authoritative opinions but rather versatile rules that advance with the moving tides of society. The family considers how values become a wellspring of strength, giving a structure to moral navigation, cultivating solidarity in variety, and shaping the family's reaction to challenges. In the reflection on values, the family comprehends that the heritage passed down isn't simply a bunch of standards however a unique power that shapes its personality and characterizes the aggregate ethos.

Intelligence, as a fundamental part of the family's inheritance, unfurls as an embroidery woven with the strings of involvement, reflection, and shared bits of knowledge. The family ponders the examples learned through preliminaries and wins, the tales that convey the refined insight of older folks, and the pearls of understanding that have been gone down through ages. In the thought of shrewdness, the family discovers that it isn't bound to progress in years yet courses through the shared mindset, molding choices, cultivating flexibility, and giving an establishment to development. The family considers how insight turns into a wellspring of congruity, interfacing the past with the present, and offering a reference point of direction for what's in store. In the reflection on shrewdness, the family comprehends that the heritage passed down isn't simply a store of information yet a living power that enhances its story with profundity and keenness.

Aggregate encounters, interlaced into the family's inheritance, arise as stories that tight spot ages together. The family considers the common victories that have become wellsprings of motivation, the difficulties that have tried its grit, and the achievements that imprint its process through time. In the thought of aggregate encounters, the family discovers that they are not disconnected occurrences but rather sections in a bigger story — a story that rises above individual lives and makes a common feeling of character. The family considers how aggregate encounters become a common heartbeat, reverberating through time and interfacing the strings of its story. In the reflection on aggregate encounters, the family comprehends that the heritage passed down isn't simply a progression of occasions yet a living story that shapes its character with the immortal beauty of shared history.

Heritage transmission, as the family mulls over its deliberate passing down, turns into a significant demonstration of association between ages. The family thinks about the purposeful work to move values, customs, intelligence, and aggregate encounters from older folks to more youthful individuals. In the thought of heritage transmission, the family discovers that it isn't simply an exchange of information however a corresponding trade that improves both the provider and the beneficiary. The family considers how purposeful inheritance transmission turns into a scaffold between the insight of the past and the capability representing things to come, encouraging a feeling of congruity and guaranteeing that the familial story stays energetic and important. In the reflection on heritage transmission, the family comprehends that the demonstration of passing down inheritance is certainly not a one-time event yet a consistent exchange that shapes the continuous story of familial personality.

As the family digs further into the thought of heritage, it perceives that heritage is certainly not a static substance yet a powerful power that shapes its personality, impacts its decisions, and gives a feeling of rootedness in a quickly impacting world. The family discovers that heritage isn't bound to stupendous signals however is in many cases tracked down in the ordinary ceremonies, the little thoughtful gestures, and the common snapshots of bliss that aggregate over the long run. In the reflection on heritage, the family comprehends that it isn't simply a beneficiary of past impacts however a functioning member in molding the inheritance it will pass down to people in the future.

The thought of heritage welcomes the family to be purposeful in its activities, aware of the effect every choice and decision can have on the story that will be acquired by ensuing ages. The family ponders the obligation that accompanies being caretakers of heritage, perceiving that it isn't simply an individual belonging yet a common trust that rises above individual lifetimes. In the consideration of heritage, the family discovers that it isn't simply a beneficiary of a legacy however a supporter of a continuous story — a story that is formed by decisions today and the qualities maintained in the present.

7.3 Final thoughts on the enduring power of collective strength and shared joy.

As we stand at the junction of reflection, looking back upon the multifaceted embroidered artwork of familial accounts woven with strings of aggregate strength and shared satisfaction, last contemplations arise — significant bits of knowledge into the persevering through force of these interlaced powers that have molded the family's excursion. In the material of familial encounters, aggregate strength remains as a foundation, a tough establishment whereupon the family has endured storms, explored difficulties, and arose victorious. At the same time, shared satisfaction, similar to a brilliant sun, has enlightened the haziest corners of difficulty, projecting a warm shine that rises above individual minutes and ties the family together in an embroidery of affection and association.

Aggregate strength, the quiet power that joins hearts and braces spirits, has appeared in the family's reaction to challenges. It isn't only the amount of individual limits however a synergistic energy that emerges when hearts thump as one. The family considers how, in snapshots of wellbeing emergencies, monetary difficulties, and outer disturbances, the aggregate strength turned into a reference point of flexibility, changing obstructions into potential open doors for development. In wellbeing emergencies, the family found that the consolidated help, sympathy, and shared assurance turned into a recuperating demulcent that rose above the constraints of clinical vulnerabilities.

Monetary difficulties, once saw as obstacles, became venturing stones as the family pooled assets, shared liabilities, and explored the complex dance of monetary limitations together. The reflection on monetary difficulties uncovers that aggregate strength isn't just about enduring financial tempests yet about tracking down clever fixes, adjusting to change, and epitomizing the soul of shared liability. In outside disturbances, whether as cataclysmic events or cultural movements, the family's aggregate reaction turned into a story of fortitude, local area influence, and an affirmation of its interconnectedness with the more extensive world.

Shared euphoria, a brilliant power woven into the familial story, turns into a demonstration of the family's capacity to track down snapshots of joy in the midst of the intricacies of life. The family considers festivities, customs, and shared encounters that have become supplies of happiness, cultivating a positive climate and making enduring recollections.

In snapshots of shared euphoria, the family discovers that bliss isn't simply a singular pursuit yet an aggregate undertaking — a common chuckling that reverberations through time, making a feeling of harmony and solidarity.

Customs, woven with the brilliant strings of aggregate strength and shared satisfaction, stand as support points that maintain the familial character. The family considers how customs, whether went down through ages or made once again, become snapshots of association, coherence, and shared importance. In the reflection on customs, the family comprehends that they are not simple ceremonies but rather living articulations of shared values, aggregate strength, and the getting through force of harmony. Customs become a demonstration of the family's obligation to saving a feeling of personality, cultivating solidarity, and making an inheritance that rises above individual lifetimes.

The excursion of aggregate strength and shared euphoria stretches out past the commonplace and normal, contacting the significant and holy parts of life. In snapshots of sorrow and misfortune, the family's aggregate strength turns into a consoling hug, and shared happiness turns into a recognition for the recollections of left friends and family. The family thinks about how, even with individual emergencies and social difficulties, the getting through obligations of aggregate strength and shared euphoria become wellsprings of comfort, recuperating, and development.

Instructive and vocation pursuits, frequently set apart by individual goals, become reflections on the aggregate strength got from familial consolation, support, and shared triumphs. The family thinks about how individual victories are not secluded accomplishments but rather aggregate victories that add to the account of shared delight. In the reflection on instructive and profession pursuits, the family discovers that the quest for individual objectives turns into an excursion of aggregate strengthening, where every part's accomplishments add to the aggregate strength and shared delight of the whole family.

Innovation, frequently seen as a device that interfaces yet may likewise detach, turns into a reflection on the family's capacity to saddle its true capacity for aggregate strength and shared delight. The family discovers that deliberate utilization of innovation makes spans across geological distances, cultivating correspondence, sharing encounters, and supporting familial securities in the computerized domain. In the reflection on innovation, the family comprehends that the persevering through power lies in the gadgets as well as in the purposeful development of associations that improve the texture of aggregate strength and shared delight.

The deliberate correspondence that supports aggregate strength and shared delight turns into a reflection on the profundity of understanding that arises through open exchanges. The family ponders how purposeful discussions make a space where weaknesses are embraced, misconceptions are explained, and love is communicated in words as well as in the demonstration of tuning in.

In the reflection on purposeful correspondence, the family comprehends that the persevering through power lies in the nature of discussions that reinforce familial bonds and add to the common repository of bliss.

The purposeful production of shared spaces, both physical and profound, turns into a reflection on the family's capacity to cultivate harmony. The family examines how shared spaces become safe-havens where aggregate strength is sustained, and shared bliss is developed. Whether in the glow of a family home or in the hug of shared customs, the family discovers that the deliberate production of shared spaces turns into an establishment for persevering through associations that endure the everyday hardships.

The thought of the inheritance went down through ages turns into a significant reflection on the persevering through force of aggregate strength and shared bliss. The family considers how customs, values, shrewdness, and aggregate encounters have molded its character and turned into a wellspring of solidarity in the midst of difficulties. In the reflection on heritage, the family comprehends that the persevering through power lies in the legacy as well as in the deliberate transmission of aggregate strength and shared happiness starting with one age then onto the next.

As the family closes its pondering excursion through the maze of aggregate strength and shared satisfaction, the last considerations reverberation with a resonating truth — the persevering through force of these powers lies not in detachment but rather in their harmonious dance. Aggregate strength and shared satisfaction are not discrete substances but rather interweaved strings that make a strong texture, an embroidery that catches the pith of familial bonds. In the last contemplations, the family embraces the acknowledgment that the getting through force of aggregate strength and shared delight isn't simply a component of its excursion yet the very heartbeat that heartbeats through the story of harmony. As the family looks toward the future, it conveys with it the insight earned from reflections, the flexibility developed through difficulties, and the significant comprehension that in aggregate strength and shared euphoria, there is a wellspring of getting through adoration that rises above existence — an adoration that ties the family in a strong hug, guaranteeing that its process keeps on unfurling with the commitment of shared skylines and blissful fellowship.